The
JONAH
Complex

Rediscovering the
Outrageous Grace of God

GREG HASLAM

RIVER
PUBLISHING

River Publishing & Media Ltd
Barham Court
Teston
Maidstone
Kent
ME18 5BZ
United Kingdom

info@river-publishing.co.uk

ISBN 978-1-908393-04-3
Printed in the United Kingdom

Contents

Dedication

To the passionate and compassionate members
of Westminster Chapel, London, whom
God has formed into a loving family of
close friends and joyful fellow-workers for Christ.

Together we've experienced God's outrageous grace
in revealing Christ's love to us, then firing us with
the Holy Spirit's zeal to make Jesus widely known
in our "Nineveh" of London.

"And who knows whether you have not come
to the kingdom for such a time as this?"
(Esther 4:14, ESV)

Acknowledgements

My warmest thanks to Tim Pettingale, my Editor at River Publishing. We have worked together on two previous projects and I've always been encouraged by his enthusiasm, constructive feedback and efficiency in helping turn the spoken word into written prose, whilst making it all look fairly effortless – which it most certainly isn't.

Thanks also to my friend and predecessor at Westminster Chapel, Dr R.T. Kendall, to whom I owe an incalculable debt for the influence his ministry has had upon my wife and me since we first met him and attended Westminster Chapel during two years of theological training at the London Theological Seminary, beginning in the Autumn of 1978. I am grateful to him for consenting to write the Foreword to this book on Jonah, not least because he published his first book, a series of sermons on Jonah himself in 1978, and though I have not read it again since then it has lastingly affected me due to his freshness and originality. If there is any overlap with his work after all these years, it is not so much plagiarism on my part, but evidence of the impact R.T. Kendall's preaching has on anyone who has ever had the privilege of hearing him speak or reading him in print.

I also honour the members of my close and loving family, including my extraordinary wife Ruth; my three wonderful sons, James, Andrew, and Joshua; along with their equally special wives - Emily, Sie Yan and Jenny. Their loving support and joyful banter bring me tremendous pleasure and help keep me sane with their raucous fun and playful humour - another evidence of God's outrageous grace in our lives. Thank you James, for diligently proof-reading the script of this book, in spite of the fact that in the same month your wife Emily gave birth to our third grandchild,

Felix. I trust he will grow up to be a very happy child and bring much happiness to many lives, just as his name so beautifully indicates and prophetically predicts.

Finally, my gratitude to all at River Publishing for your support of this project, and especially to Stefan Proudfoot for his creative artwork and striking cover design.

Greg Haslam,
Westminster Chapel, London,
December 2011

Foreword

Sometimes people ask me, "Why did you choose Greg Haslam to be your successor at Westminster Chapel?" My answer has always been the same: it was clear to me then (ten years ago) and now. I had two major criteria in my search for a successor: (1) a man who was truly reformed in theology and (2) one who is absolutely open and comfortable with the "immediate and direct" (to quote Dr Martyn Lloyd-Jones) witness of the Holy Spirit. Therefore to seek for someone who is dedicated to the sovereignty of God and the immediate witness of the Holy Spirit is to look for a combination that is exceedingly rare.

But I now have yet another answer to people who might ask why I chose Greg: *read this book*. It speaks for itself. It makes me look good! Here is a volume that is both learned and easy to read. It is well researched and yet inspiring. Greg's treatment of the book of Jonah also provides important background knowledge regarding the book of Jonah. I love the fact that Greg not only exudes integrity from start to the finish but maintains a robust and unashamed conviction regarding the God of the Old Testament. Here is a word that needs to be shouted around the world: the God of the Old Testament and the God of the New Testament is the one same true eternal God. Not only that; Greg upholds the view that the story of Jonah is literally true – a position so many modern scholars seem embarrassed to affirm.

When Greg asked me if I would write the Foreword to this book, I replied: "Oh, I know it will be a good book – you will be copying me and all I have written in my own book, Jonah; you will have plagiarized the whole thing word for word!" I hoped he would laugh. He did. But now for a further observation: his book is better than mine. It deserves to be written. And read. His book will be in print long after mine is out of print. Do not be surprised when he refers to me; it was a kind thing for him to do. But he has done a masterful job, having produced a piece of work that deserves to be read by every church leader and every believer.

Greg Haslam is devoted not only to preaching but also to the prophetic ministry. It is one of his main emphases; he is absolutely at home with it. He therefore has an appreciation for both the man Jonah as well as the book of Jonah. Greg consequently has written a book that gives a relevance and a perspective often missed by some scholars who comment on the book of Jonah and yet never get it!

I therefore commend what follows and pray that your mind will be challenged and your heart warmed by what you are about to read. May you be edified and the God of the Bible glorified.

Dr R.T. Kendall

Introduction

"Now the word of the Lord came to Jonah the son of Amittai, saying, 'Arise, go to Nineveh, that great city, and call out against it, for their evil has come up before me.' But Jonah rose to flee to Tarshish from the presence of the Lord. He went down to Joppa and found a ship going to Tarshish. So he paid the fare and went down into it, to go with them to Tarshish, away from the presence of the Lord."

The story of Jonah is one of the best known in the Bible and the least understood. In its simplest form, it's a staple favourite of Sunday School teachers everywhere. For that reason alone we tend to think we know the story well, but in fact there is much more than meets the child-like eye when we begin to dig more deeply beneath the surface. Although Jonah's biblical account is short – just 4 chapters and less than 60 verses in total – it packs a powerful prophetic punch. It imparts a life-changing impact on those who take its message seriously. The central message of Jonah is simple and clear: the Lord God has a passion for reaching the unreached that's bigger than ours. He has a commitment to evangelism that far exceeds our own. Daily, He seeks to reach out to those who live in ignorance of His love and grace – and He is committed to doing so through His people. Amazingly, even in the light of God's painful experience with His reluctant prophet-evangelist Jonah, God still insists on reaching the world through the agency of His Church. We are not bypassed. He calls and recruits us but often has to rebuke our guilty silence.

So the book of Jonah is ultimately the success story of God the Evangelist. Even when His people let Him down badly, God never fails! But Jonah's story is more than that. It is a deeply instructive health-check and CAT-scan for our souls. It carries many lessons about God's relationship and dealings with us. I found studying Jonah's life full of startling surprises, deeply penetrating, enormously challenging, but encouraging and inspiring too. As you read on may your experience be the same.

Greg Haslam
Westminster Chapel, London, 2011

1. Hard to Swallow

The book of Jonah stands out as markedly different from its companions amongst the twelve minor prophets. To begin with, it is the only book written as a narrative. Its prophetic message is unusually wrapped up in its storytelling delivery. Normally, biblical prophecy is given to us through declaration and proclamation, but here the prophetic message is delivered in its entirety as the tale of Jonah unfolds. Because of its unique content and genre, one might well ask, "What am I to do with this book?"

It's a good question. Historically, the message of Jonah has been interpreted in a variety of different ways. Early Christians were struck by the typological similarities between Jonah and Jesus, especially due to Christ's own reference to the story, highlighting the parallel between Jonah's experience in the belly of the fish and His own predicted three-day burial prior to His resurrection (Matthew 12:40-41).

Some have seen Jonah as a kind of negative stereotype of the Jews. Jonah seemed to embody the kind of xenophobia, exclusivity and lack of compassion that has sometimes characterised Jewish hearts towards their gentile neighbours. From John Calvin onwards, many have viewed Jonah as a warning to Christians against trying to resist God's purposes and "run away" from Him – and against devaluing the very people who God is trying to reach.

Still others have dismissed Jonah as "non-literal". They argue that it is just an extended parable, fable or didactic novel. Proponents of this view insist that it is not an historical account so much as a satirical work, intended to highlight the spiritual prejudices that have marked the people of God in every generation.

But while sceptics have ridiculed the supernatural phenomena the book describes, others have defended it for its historicity, its truth-telling and its miracles. I belong to this latter category. My confident conviction is that, if Christ treated Jonah as a living, historical figure and the events of his life as real historical events, then so should we. So we work from a position of belief, rather than doubt. We are setting out to examine an authentic, historical record containing grounded, historical truth. As such, the story of Jonah carries a message for God's people in all times and in all places – because what happened to Jonah can happen to us.

A book of four themes

Perhaps the best approach to understanding the message of Jonah is to focus on its four major themes, which unfold along with the narrative:

• *It teaches us about God's generous grace.* This results in both divine and human repentance. In the story we see Jonah's repentance and, of course, Nineveh's repentance, but God also relents and changes His mind. This fact in itself provides us with a further conundrums which provoke our thoughts and press us for solutions.

• *The puzzle of unfulfilled prophecy.* We read of Jonah prophesying, "Yet forty days and Nineveh will be overthrown" (Jonah 3:4), but that outcome didn't happen historically for another twenty years. This is a puzzle that demands our attention.

• *The exposure of Jewish attitudes to gentiles in mission.* In doing so, it demands that the contemporary Church awakens to her calling too, so that we don't repeat Jonah's mistake ourselves, dismissing some people groups as beyond help.

• *Its strange defence or theodicy for God's just government over His world.* It justifies God's actions in the affairs of world history. People are constantly questioning what God is up to, seeking to understand the puzzling decisions they believe He makes, whilst we look for answers to different situations in the world. The book of Jonah doesn't explain everything to us, but it does throw light on the fact of God's ongoing involvement in world history.

One thing is certain here. You cannot read the book of Jonah carefully without being profoundly affected by it. Chapter 1 parallels chapter 3 as a non-Israelite audience (first the sailors on the vessel Jonah travels on, then the tens of thousands of Ninevites) are confronted with the reality and power of God leading to amazing results – their conversion in both cases.

Then chapters 2 and 4 are similarly parallel as God has to deal with His own people before He can touch the nations around them – perhaps the main reason why the content becomes so personally challenging for us as we read.

A provocative book

In summary, one could say that Jonah's message is both *provocative* and *prophetic*. If we, as the Church, are on the move, eager to fulfil our mandate and mission, then there are many things that are essential for us to both experience and avoid. Let's ponder some of them under these two broad headings without, at this point, seeking definitive answers.

1. It addresses us personally

More than thirty years ago, Dr RT Kendall began his ministry at Westminster Chapel with an expository sermon series on the book of Jonah. Back then he was studying for his PhD at Oxford University and wasn't initially the pastor of the church – he was simply filling in for a prolonged period, the church helping him as he helped the church. He travelled regularly from Oxford to preach in London and had planned a series of eight messages, but this eventually expanded into twenty-one messages. Halfway through the series the Deacons approached him and asked him, on behalf of the church, to become their pastor.

Perhaps RT arbitrarily chose the subject of Jonah as a challenging book for a London church. But he soon realised it was more significant. Then, and over the years since, he has said of himself, "I am Jonah!" - because he never intended to remain ministering in the UK as long as he did. London was his Nineveh in that respect. For very similar reasons, this piece of history personalises the theme of Jonah for me. Positioned as we are in a populous megacity, it begs the question: *are things now better or worse for us in London thirty-five years on?*

Allow the message of Jonah to provoke you with a similar question: take a look back into your history and take stock. Examine your church's life with God. Examine your personal growth in maturity as a believer. Are things better now than they were then, or has there been a static standstill or steady decline? Are you closer in intimacy with God than you were? Are you more closely aligned with His plans and purposes or further away from them? Try not to answer these questions too quickly. In taking a personal inventory, think about the choices and paths you have taken that have led you to where you are now.

2. It speaks to us in our locality

The second provocative challenge of Jonah inevitably comes as we examine its context. Here was Jonah, sent to a large, populous, predominantly pagan city to proclaim God's word. The challenge to us is this: will we fare any better in our mission than Jonah did? Or will we renege on our responsibilities and calling to the degree that God will have to mete out similar treatment to us, if He is going to see us fulfil our destiny? Are we reluctant prophets of God? Do we fully understand the consequences of not doing as we're told? Again, don't answer that enquiry too quickly!

3. It disrupts our personal peace and affluence

It is self-evident that personal peace and affluence are not the themes of Jonah's story, but they are often the priority themes and goals of many Christian lives today. Ideally, believers would like to live comfortable, blessed lives and then be transported to heaven at the end with the minimum of hassle in between. But Jonah speaks of an entirely different trajectory God may have planned for us. The Hebrew word *ra'ah* is used throughout the text. It is applied to both Jonah and Nineveh in the narrative to describe what happened to them and is translated respectively "discomfort" and "destruction". Nineveh was threatened with destruction, and Jonah experienced great personal discomfort.

The question is, will God have to discomfort us so that our "Nineveh", whatever that means to us, will not be destroyed? And can both these things be averted by our actions? Are we here on this planet for an easy life, or are we serious about being used by God – even if there is a considerable cost attached to willing co-operation with Him?

4. It examines our hearts

The last provocation of Jonah digs deeper still beneath the surface of our lives. It asks, what is our heart towards others who are very different from us? To contextualise this, let's ask what is our heart attitude towards Muslims, immigrants, criminals, the homeless, militant atheists, and many who live on the fringes of our society? Do we love them or feel disdain towards them? Do we exercise compassion towards those who live outside of Christ or quietly ignore them? Do we pity plants more than we pity people? Do we want to "save the whale" or save the lost? In short, is there anyone in our thinking who is beyond God's mercy? Or does His mercy, working through us, have a boundless reach that transcends our limiting prejudices? Doesn't His grace show up in some of the most surprising places and do the most amazing things?

These are important, provocative questions. If we want to know what the Church will look like a decade from now – if we want to assess what impact it is likely to have – then these questions lie at the heart of the matter. This is what the book of Jonah is all about. God is raising some vitally important issues for us to consider.

A prophetic book

Jonah is a provocative book because it is a *prophetic* book. It is not just an instructive morality tale – God Himself is speaking to us through this narrative. In the Old Testament the prophet was

God's mouthpiece. The New Testament makes clear that we as God's people are the living organs and limbs of Christ's body on earth, through which He is able to enact His will in the lives of those around us. We are His hands, His feet, and we can often express His heart as well. But prophets are supremely God's mouthpiece, and the "eyes and ears of the Church".

Prophets speak out things that we don't naturally know – and sometimes don't want to know! They regularly tell both the Church and the world things that neither of them want to hear. Their mouths got them into big trouble in the Old Testament, but equally, their mouths got other people out of big trouble – people like the Ninevites. Prophets can access a hotline to God and sometimes extend a lifeline from God. If the message of Jonah can be taken and read personally in our context, then we need to realise this: God doesn't want to deal harshly with us in bringing us into line with His will, so He throws us a lifeline in sending prophetic people to us – something we can reach for and grab. But we won't be rescued and we won't be changed unless we listen to what the prophet is saying.

1. Prophets unveil to us the mind of God

In order to do God's will, of course, we have to know God's mind. We can't second-guess what God is up to or run ahead of Him presumptuously. Frequently, God will use the prophetic word of choice messengers to express His heart to us – especially if we are going off-track and are out of line with His Word.

Prophets remind us of what God's will is. They reveal His mind to us. Their words are not just titbits of titillating information that cause us to say, "That's interesting, I never knew that before…" Anchored in timeless scriptural revelation from the Bible, they are more likely to be the deliverers of life-changing words related to our calling and destiny. Our lives need not drizzle away one day at a time, wastefully expended on trivia. Instead, we can discover God's plan for us and invest our lives wisely in order to bring God and us a great return on His investment.

Prophets see what others cannot see, and dare to say what others dare not say. Every prophetic word needs to be carefully weighed and considered, tested by the supreme authority of scripture, but we would do well to take such words seriously and listen for the voice of God in what we hear. We need to understand that God is speaking to us through Jonah, so that his ancient message can again impact our contemporary world.

2. Prophets disclose to us the heart of God

Through the prophetic word we "catch" something not only of what God thinks about things, but how He feels about them too. Catching the heart of God makes us feel different as a result; it changes us. Notice that in Scripture many of the prophetic writings are presented in the form of poetry, not prose. Prose is the language of the intellect; poetry is an expression of the heart. In prose, we are often detached, so that words are our servants doing our will. But in being exposed to poetry, words become our masters, moving us to address heart-issues and even change direction.

Proverbs 4:23 says, "Keep your heart with all diligence, for from it flow the springs of life." God knows what is going on in our hearts and therefore what is going to come out in our lives. That's why He wants to profoundly affect our hearts. Only those whose hearts are open to God's heart will fully understand what the prophet is saying. As we listen we begin to understand what is hurting God's heart, what is trying His patience, what stirs Him to be merciful, even what changes His mind. We need to allow

Jonah's message to touch our emotions with the deep feelings of God, so that it affects our choices and actions too. If our top commitments in life are no different after reading Jonah, then we have not yet begun to experience God's heart.

3. Prophets help us to read and understand the times

The Old Testament prophets lived in eras of great turmoil and great pressure, much like our own times. They saw periods of political crises, conflict, and spiritual disaster. They were aware of sin and decay in troubled communities around them. They observed the real causes behind the alarming decline of civilisations breaking apart across their planet, just as we observe such events today. That is why we will never read an "out-of-date" biblical prophet. Reading them is like holding up a mirror to our own times and our own lives – we cannot help but see our reflection or identikit picture in their words.

Often this is not a comfortable experience. As GK Chesterton wrote, "I don't want a church that tells me when I am right; I want a church that tells me when I am wrong." God tells us accurately what is wrong with us then gives us grace to put it right.

Chesterton was exhorting the Church to stop trying to accommodate current fads and foolishness in misguided attempts to be politically correct, to stop being the lap dog of the God-defying shapers of the status quo. He wanted to see a Church that truly had a voice to its world, and could express God's heart and mind clearly. God has something very important to say to us through Jonah, so we need to listen carefully and marinate in what we hear.

An invitation to enter the story

Bible stories are amazing for their brevity. Unlike the 500-page thriller novels one can find on bookstands at airports or train stations, the main characteristic of a biblical story is it's tight narrative brevity, and suggestive succinctness. The sentences are short, its descriptions sparse. There are not many adjectives, just efficient provocative reportage.

In Jonah there is a similar reticence to fill in all the details that we might like. The chapters are austere, inconclusive, even open-ended, as loose ends go unaddressed and unresolved. The end of the book leaves us asking the question, "Yes, I've been drawn in by the drama and suspense, but what happened next?" Did Jonah go back into Nineveh? What happened to Nineveh? What was its long-term fate? We just don't know.

There is a good reason why God leaves all of this hanging in the air. It is His invitation for you and I to enter into the story ourselves, just as we are and as best as we can. More important than the missing details is the question we are continually forced to ask ourselves while reading: "Could I be Jonah? Could God be talking to me?" God's intention is for us to engage with this story and allow ourselves to be transformed by its message. The questions we have are not as important as the outcome they lead to in our lives.

Hard to swallow?

As we engage with the details of Jonah's story in the following chapters, please lay aside any childhood Sunday School images of Jonah safely ensconced like Disney's runaway cartoon character Pinocchio inside the whale, that may be lurking inside your head. This is not an amusing entertainment irrelevant to adult real-life experiences. Jonah's life, like our lives, was a bit more complex than that. Some find his story hard to swallow – as hard to swallow as the giant fish must have found Jonah to be! But the Bible has all the answers we need to our enquiries, as well as all the right questions we need to ask in the first place.

As we continue, please meditate on the truths that are uncovered. The Hebrew word for meditate is *hagah* – a word used of a lion growling over the prey in its mouth or a dog chewing on a bone, sucking all the marrow out of it. It takes time to chew and then ingest hard truth, but it is always worth the effort. God wants us to be like a "dog with a bone" where His truth is concerned, until it breaks down into digestible morsels and seeps into our very souls to feed and change our lives. Chew over the story of Jonah and draw out of it all that God wants.

In several places in Scripture God's servants are commanded to "eat" His word (see Revelation 10:1-4; 8-10; Jeremiah 15:16; Ezekiel 2:8, 3:3). The implication is that His word is to be eaten slowly in manageable bites, then chewed over thoughtfully to be thoroughly digested. Jonah is not just a book to make notes upon then file away. By all means make notes, but don't just make notes! Prepare your heart to allow this book to have its full impact on your life.

Beyond its personal impact on us there is, I believe, a much larger agenda here, in that God desires to re-envision and mobilise His Church. God is using this stunning message of Jonah today to accomplish His purposes so that, in due course, all Heaven will be let loose on earth, so that earth will look more and more like Heaven. When God speaks, things happen!

What may God do with our lives through the message of Jonah? Who knows? But however hard to swallow some may find this story to be, let's imbibe its truth and remain attentive to the Holy Spirit's voice. After all, you are what you eat.

2. The Power of One
(Jonah 1:1-2)

As narrative history, the book of Jonah is one of the best known in the Bible. Although not a children's story, it nevertheless contains evocative, sometimes disturbing images that grab the attention of young and old alike, sucking them into an encounter with the shocking realities of a life without God. Few books possess it's power to penetrate and possess the reader until its work is accomplished in our lives, much as God dealt with wayward Jonah himself.

There is an old saying, "Better to light a candle than curse the darkness." If any nation on earth had reason to curse the existence of Nineveh it was Israel, and so if any individual had reason to curse Nineveh it was Jonah. This city was the capital of Assyria, the enemy of Israel since the days of the destruction of the Israelite northern kingdom in 721BC.

The people of Nineveh lived life without boundaries or any kind of moral framework, and had spiralled into lawlessness and carnality, paganism and evil. It is into the backdrop of this darkness and depravity that God asks Jonah to enter and light a candle. This is difficult if a tornado of resistance is all you are likely to encounter.

The commitment of God

The book of Jonah is rich with the message of God's faithfulness. As we read it, it will enlarge our view of the extent to which He is prepared to interact with His world in order to turn lives around.

• *It shows us that God is deeply affected by human sin.* Unlike the remote gods of the philosophers and false theologians, God is not indifferent to sin. Neither does He indulge in it, as did the gods of the pagans, who immersed themselves in the same depravity as morally corrupt human beings. God is without sin (2 Corinthians 5:21) and from Genesis to Revelation, the Bible shows Him to be both incensed by sin and intolerant of it. His pain is infinitely deeper than our own, and yet, in response to the sinner, His mercy is fully and freely available.

• *It reveals that God has power to wipe out whole cities.* Jonah was instructed to declare to the city of Nineveh that it had forty days remaining before it would completely obliterated (Jonah 3:4). This is not always an easy concept for us to grasp. We feel much more comfortable encountering a benign and benevolent God than a God who can permit drought, plagues, economic and natural disasters. The reality is that because He is ultimately loving, God will sometimes let loose the reins that hold us back in order to expose us to the consequences of our own choices, not just as individuals but as nations. This is the God of the Bible: it is the way He has worked at different points in history in order to get the attention His people, in order to awaken those who are not.

• *We see that God is in complete and sovereign control of everything.* From the tiniest microcosm of the workings of the human cell to the complex macrocosm of the movements of galaxies in space, God is in control of His creation. He is not the distant and semi-retired god of the deists. He is still the interventionist God of the Bible. The book of Jonah reveals His involvement in the workings of worms, whales, the weather, wayward prophets and wicked cities. He is at work in both small and great things for the ultimate good of those He has called (Romans 8:28).

• *It highlights that God can act in isolation, but He prefers interaction.* If He wanted to, God could have suddenly and without warning, wiped out Nineveh with a flick of His finger, totally destroying it forever. But instead He chose Jonah as His agent for change. God is relational. The Bible is full of accounts of the partnership between God and men, women and children, who are given the mandate to implement His will on the earth as it is fully obeyed in heaven. The same is true for the Church today. God loves to employ human agency.

• *It teaches us that God's word changes destinies.* When His word is put in the right mouth, spoken authentically and with reverence, it carries unlimited weight and power. Far from being a transient puff of air or ineffective watery sentiment, God's prophetic word knows no limit as it ripples and splashes onto thirsty ground. Through the power of one, the destiny of Nineveh was changed forever, and throughout the generations, God has always sought those who would be His mouthpiece to bring about lasting change.

Introducing the cast

In chapter 1 verses 1-2 we are introduced to the main players in the narrative, and to the striking call of God upon which the book is based. Contained within just 4 chapters, less than 60 verses, this succinct, seductive and haunting tale has captured the imagination of Christians who, for generations, have devoured its meaning and been energized by its message.

The three main characters at the hub of the story, Nineveh, God and Jonah, are the players that capture the most interest, but the peripheral bit parts, played out by the great fish, swarthy sailors and a troublesome worm, all season this tale with spicy incidents as well, adding to it's flavour.

1. Nineveh

The city of Nineveh was the terrifying capital of the aggressive emerging Empire of Assyria, and deserved to be wiped off the map. In the book of Jonah, there are no elaborate descriptions of the buildings contained within it or the landscape that surrounded it. Nineveh could offer nothing to the accidental tourist, and unlike the written rhetoric of a glossy travel brochure, the description of the city in the biblical narrative is sparse and grey. The extent to which Nineveh had sunk, propelled it into the depths of decadence, terror, exploitation and hateful violence. It was now well advanced as a city in dire jeopardy: dangerous, unpredictable and unsafe. Situated in the desert area we now know as Iran and Iraq, it stood as a symbol of all future nations who refuse to acknowledge the God of Israel as the only true God, and turn to false gods that corrupt its life from within.

Nevertheless, Nineveh still existed under the final control of God, because as the author of all creation, He is neither limited to one tribe, nor is He constrained by any national boundaries. The whole world is His, and He holds all nations equally accountable to Himself, whether they acknowledge this or not. God-denying, it declined into pitiless cruelty and vicious militaristic ambitions for ruthless conquest.

The book of Jonah creaks under the weighty tension of how God can, at the same time, be both angry with and concerned about the condition of Nineveh. The people who lived there were a part of the world He loved and still loves, despite participating in perverse thinking and suicidal sin, which He considers utterly abhorrent. Paradoxically, He was both ready to deal harshly with Nineveh and show mercy to it by sending Jonah as His prophet, with the intent of saving it. 2 Peter 3:9 says, "The Lord is not slow to fulfil His promise as some count slowness, but is patient toward you, not wishing that any should perish, but that all should reach repentance." Jonah then becomes the key person to reverse God's righteous judgement on an idolatrous nation, if he can first reverse their cruelty, despicable idolatry and escalating aggression towards the nations. It is a vivid illustration of the power of one!

This is an important theme for us in the 21st century. Nineveh characterizes the vast majority of the nations of our world who marginalise God from their systems of government, national laws and religion. We have become desensitized to the dangers of life without God, and embraced rival and competitive worldviews.

Do we ever take time to feel how God feels about the exploitation of the poor, the escalating impact of domestic and international violence, the unravelling of the family unit? Or like Jonah, do we want to run away from the onerous and unpopular responsibility of communicating His urgent call for nations and individuals to repent?

Are we unwilling to sacrifice our comfortable lives for the sake of Christ and endangered people whom He loves, when He has so solemnly told us to go into the entire world and preach the gospel (Matthew 28:18-20)?

Our world has changed radically since September 2001. The collapse of New York's Twin Towers shook the world, and spread the contagion of the unclean fear of man, but did not accelerate the clean fear of God. We are reminded daily of the threat of local and global radical extremism which can, like a vice, grip the heart with dread if we let it. Whilst we need to remain vigilant of course, the real danger is not from bomb threats or the release of immigrant criminals from prison; it is that we have forgotten God. We no longer hold fast to His laws and His love; instead we have tolerated wickedness and ceased to detest it in the way He does. Like Nineveh, our cities deserve His judgement, but with Jonah, we are summoned to preach and cry out for the possibility of His mercy and forgiveness to a world fast ripening for judgement.

2. God

The prophecies of the Old Testament can prove to be a puzzle to us. In our ever-changing world, with it's technological advancements and increasing sophistication, where can we find continuity of meaning in the present with God's messages of old? What is an appropriate hermeneutic?

Over the centuries, theologians have struggled to define the relationship between the Old and New Testament in the light of the coming of Jesus Christ. One such extreme example was the ancient heresy birthed by Marcion in the 2nd century who completely rejected the God of the Old Testament as a malevolent creator, whom Jesus came to destroy. In his view, everything that had been recorded prior to the birth of Jesus was irrelevant and defunct, including the messages of the canonical prophets. Sadly, in some quarters, this heresy is still active today.

The truth is this: our God, as revealed in Scripture, is the same God of both the Old and New Testaments. Everything we read in the Old Testament about God remains true for all time, and can be received intact and should not be altered, as our Lord never changes. The message of Jonah is the message for today. If Nineveh was in danger from the wrath of God, then so are cities like London, Manchester, Glasgow, New York, Beijing and Moscow.

Yet it is surprising how little authentic fear of God can be found in these cities today, and even within the churches within these cities. We neither fear God's anger, nor hope for His mercy, as we can and as we should.

God is the main character in the book of Jonah. The account of how He sets about recreating and restoring the broken city of Nineveh is breathtaking. Is this not a universal theme of the commitment of God to people and cities in need of regeneration? Wherever God's word goes, His presence follows. The word that came to Jonah was a promise of His faithfulness to see the work through to completion. It was not simply a patch-up job or an emergency strategy. God wanted to clean up the city from it's core; angry at its wickedness but committed to its recovery.

Whilst I pray for the political leaders of our nation, I don't set much store by any proposed measures to protect the population from danger by way of ID cards, closed-circuit cameras or extra policing on our streets. These things may make a measurable difference, but our trust has to be in the most powerful agent for change in the universe: the word of the Lord preached in the power of His Spirit. God created the world by His word (Genesis 1). It is His word that delivers, heals, recreates, and restores both men and nations. Just as "The word of the Lord came to Jonah…" and just as Jesus spoke life into the centurion's sick servant from a distance of seven miles away (Luke 7), I earnestly desire the same heavenly transactions to be repeated in our world today. Wherever God's word goes, God Himself goes with it. This is our greatest hope for national recovery and renewal.

3. Jonah

When God is planning a special mission or startling outcome, He always has His emissaries waiting in the wings. Sometimes He will use groups of people, but more often than not, it is just one individual person. As a prophet of Israel, Jonah was on-call and constant stand-by for the job, awaiting his signal and summons. In verses 1-2 of chapter 1, he is given an unusual mission that he had to choose to accept, for what the world most needs is God's word and someone genuinely called to speak it.

Jonah's mission was to expose sin and threaten God's just wrath upon it. God wanted him to communicate His warning that in forty days Nineveh would be destroyed.

Imagine the impact on Jonah!

Situations of mounting jeopardy require the arrival of a special envoy with news of an alternative outcome wherever possible. Even though God had plotted his life and was the master of it, Jonah must have wondered how on earth the wild people of the city would receive his words! Prophets have the unenviable position of rarely proving to be very popular, simply because they care more about God's word than human affirmation. A friend of mine calls prophets, "God's bogey men" – an allusion to the unsettling effects of their ministry. They may disturb and scare us sometimes, and we may not always understand them or even like them, but mostly they are messengers of God's mercy and hope.

One of the reasons Jonah was reluctant to take this message to Nineveh was that in his heart he would have known that God would want to show mercy, but in this original message to be delivered, there was not a hint of this possibility. This much is clear: Nineveh would not be saved apart from Jonah.

This is the power of one.

As Jonah moved from a position of having *no word*, to receiving a *sent word*, which was designed to be a *spoken word*, which under God's hand will become a *heard word*, from which the fruit may be an *obeyed word* and a *believed word* we see the potential for things to come. The crucial phase in this process is the place of receiving the word. Hearing God and what He has to say to us is extremely important. You may not know it yet, but God may have marked you out as His special emissary to speak His word into a situation ripe and in need of His grace and restoration. It is never easy for any of us to be called to fulfill an onerous task and it would not prove easy for Jonah. Nevertheless, God still looks for a positive response from us. Are we willing to be His agents of change? Are we ready to accept the challenge to be faithful to the call of God?

Not only does the account of the call of Jonah underline the vital necessity of mission in the Church, it above all encourages us not to discount the face of the power of one. We so easily believe the lie that we are insignificant or unimportant, but individuals count in the kingdom of God and He often uses the most unlikely people for some very important roles. One live coal can set a whole stack on fire!

Jonah was given a mighty task because God trusted him to deliver it. Jonah was given a one-way ticket to Iran, with no guarantee he would ever see home again. Despite being called "The reluctant prophet" on many occasions, he rose to the occasion as the representative of the God of the Israelites. Alec Motyer, the Old Testament scholar and theologian states, "Israel is the custodian of the whole world's welfare" and it is clear to see that as well as being a historical account, the Jonah narrative is also a parable or even paradigm for us. Jonah himself is a picture of Israel as a whole, through whom all nations would be saved by their faithfulness to God. Through Jesus, the world is now our responsibility and we are custodians of its spiritual welfare as we faithfully carry out the Great Commission Christ charged His people to advance worldwide (Matthew 28:16-20). If the nations are to move from jeopardy to deliverance and freedom, the future depends on lives like yours and mine.

Jonah's Big Commission

God is anything but indifferent to situations of moral decay. When He created mankind, God's original design was for His people to live in peace, freedom and righteousness to reflect His own nature and character. Scripture is full of God's rescue plans for His people, in both Old and New Testaments, as He draws them back to the life He intended from the very start. Throughout history, God has conscripted men and women to be His messengers into desperate situations in order to activate change.

Jonah was one such man.

1. His commission is from the Lord

Jonah had no higher calling than to be a messenger of the Lord to the city of Nineveh at that moment in time. Nothing was more important, nothing more urgent. God had chosen His man for the task and Jonah was required to speak the word of the Lord in truth so that the city would be saved.

Interestingly, the name "Jonah" means "dove" and "the son of Amittai" means "the son of truth." In scripture, the dove is not only a universal symbol of peace but also of judgement now over, and of new beginnings. In Genesis chapter 8, for instance, the dove flew back to Noah's ark with an olive branch in its beak symbolising the beginning of new life and the end of God's universal judgement after forty days of the worldwide flood. Furthermore, the dove represents the unprecedented impartation of power from the Holy Spirit upon God's people as we see from the account of the baptism of Jesus (Matthew 3).

Jonah, *the son of truth* whose name was *peace*, was commissioned by God to prophesy both His *judgement* and His *mercy*, which opened the way for a new beginning for Nineveh. This much is clear: there would be no peace until Jonah travelled there to unmask the cause of their trouble and then eradicate it.

Inevitably this commission came at the expense of a high personal cost to Jonah. The possibilities included loss of status and income, personal danger and extreme conditions. God's prophets are required to be courageous, malleable, gutsy and passionate, and so they have to learn to live with the effects of how it feels to regularly encounter the voice of God. Oswald Chambers states, "To be brought within the zone of the call of God is to be profoundly altered." The Church needs prophetic men and women to this day, in order that it does not become simply a "non-prophet organization", powerless and bland. We need those commissioned by God to speak His word into the lives of individuals, churches, cities and nations, for His kingdom to come and His will to be done on earth as it is in heaven.

2. The mark of a prophet

How do we identify a man or woman who has been commissioned by God as prophet?

i) *They have extraordinary access to God and to men.* Doors open for them both in heaven and on earth, doors that remain shut to others. This is both a privilege and a burden in the same measure. Prophetic people are able to see what others can't see and hear what others cannot hear. Then they are required to dare to say what other people will not say, answerable primarily to God for the delivery of the word and their faithfulness to Him.

ii) *Such is the presence of God in and upon prophets that unusual things happen around them.* Even when Jonah is experiencing dissonance in his relationship with God, the presence of God still crackles all around him. Approach Jonah and you will encounter storms, a big fish, a hot sirocco wind and a hungry worm. Similarly, standing in close proximity to a prophetic person today may have its surprises! They arrest attention, even when they would prefer not to, and often regardless of the mood they are in, or their own emotional or moral wellbeing at the time. Try as he might, Jonah could not remain anonymous. The same is true for prophets today, because the hand of God is upon them. The Bible tells us the gifts and calling of God are irrevocable (Romans 11:29), so they remain with us, often regardless of our mood changes and aberrant behaviour.

iii) *Prophets are men and women of passion.* Such people can be difficult to live with and even more difficult to be around! God has appointed them to carry enormous responsibility, and this comes at a price. They are prone to violent mood swings, heated prejudice, soul-searching and deep insecurity. Jonah did not always behave in a "sensible" manner because God had commissioned him for a task that was out of the ordinary, and he was required to no longer live with an earthly perspective but a heavenly one. This set him at odds with the people around him and the prevailing expectations of his time. The same is true of prophetic people today as they carry the weight of God's fresh transformational word, holding it in tension with the "normal" life they may have lived previously for a considerable time. Jonah carried responsibility for the fate of a city, which was both a great honour and an overwhelming burden.

iv) *Prophets pay a high price.* Religion that costs us nothing is worth nothing. When God calls a messenger, He asks that a man or woman come and die. Then die again and again. On the prophetic journey there will be sacrifice, criticism, ridicule, rejection and danger, and this fact alone is reason enough why so many fail to take up their intended calling. So many people, including pastors, allow the fear of the unknown to cause them to retreat into compromising a radical adventure with God in favour of a comfortable life in the safety of the harbour. God has made His Church to head out for some deep waters and to rock the boat from time to time! If Jonah had ignored his commission, God would have been denied the opportunity to use "the power of one" to restore Nineveh from the inside out. We must never settle for a life of mediocrity as followers of Christ. The high cost is always well worth it.

v) *Prophetic men and women love to serve the living God.* When He recruits His prophets, God does it within relationship. He is not the god of the atheist (who is nowhere), the god of the pantheist (who is everywhere in general but nowhere in particular), nor the god of the deist (who is always somewhere but never here right now). No, our God is immanent, relational and active. The Jonah narrative contains within it a beautiful example of the interaction between God and His prophet, who exhibits some fallen tendencies towards avoidance, fear, insecurity and procrastination but to whom God is deeply committed. This in turn draws Jonah into the place where he is willing both to listen and to serve.

Are you listening carefully to God for His call upon your life today?

3. His summons is to the city

The city of Nineveh was a proud, opportunistic and ambitious capital whose suburbs spread out as wide as sixty miles in circumference. Its imposing brick walls rose to one hundred feet and were so thick that three chariots could ride abreast on top of them. The people were noted for their engineering skills, aggressive attitude and military prowess.

However, they were also renowned for being a people of extreme cruelty and the ruthless destruction of anyone or anything that stood in their way. They flayed men alive, tied prisoners of war together with hooks through their lips and noses, cut out tongues, raped women as a sign of power, and executed people on a whim, piling their skulls up into large blood-drenched pyramids before the walls of cities laid under siege. In the book of Nahum we read an account of their cruelty and Nahum asks, "Who has not felt it?" (3:19). Who indeed!

Amazingly, though God sent Jonah to Nineveh to warn it, it was secretly and primarily to show mercy. The role of the prophet is to provoke change on a personal, communal, governmental and sometimes, national level. Jonah appears to have suspected that was God's secret intention. Even if God's message to Nineveh may not have sounded initially positive, it ultimately carried hope deep at the heart of it. Essentially, the moment a prophet of God is called to appear on the scene, there is hope released once again.

For such a call to take place, four key ingredients are required:

i) The word must be from God. God can and will express His word however He chooses. It may take the form of an audible voice, a dream, a vision, a strong impression, an engagingly constructed sentence, a specific command, a clear description, prediction or picture. What matters more than the style of it's delivery is the authenticity of it.

God can never lie: He is truth, and as His word is breathed from heaven to earth it will cut through the lies that are prevalent in our fragile, fragmented lower reality. Prophets have access to God's higher reality and it just takes one man or woman to be the instrument for change.

ii) The word has to be heard and received. When God speaks to His prophets, He wants them to listen. They act as God's mouthpiece to His deaf and dumb world. If they are dulled and numbed by the temptations and pressures of the world, it will be harder to turn people towards the purity of the word from His lips. When God spoke to Jonah in chapter 1:1-2, Jonah had already been prophesying into other situations as the Lord led him. He had a noble prior history. God did not randomly pick Jonah: He had been tested and proven as a worthy candidate to take His message to Nineveh by the way he had heard from God and spoken before. God knows our desires, and sees our commitment to a life-long journey with Him.

iii) The word has to be accurately transmitted. There is no point God speaking His word if the prophet remains sitting in the same place he first heard it! To Jonah, God says, "Arise! Go to Nineveh." (1:2), expecting that very soon, Jonah will physically arise, get up, and actually walk there. The word of God delivered from on high, has to be delivered to the people who need it *in situ* on the ground.

This journey is often a lonely road, as usually only one person is trusted with such a huge task. But God is faithful to His word and will surround the prophet-preacher with His presence and power to see that it is fully imparted, without compromise. Compromise has been defined as "Continuing to practice what you don't really believe in and learning to settle for what you don't agree with, because you lack the courage to speak up for and fight for what you really do believe in." Prophets must avoid compromise if they are to accomplish their task from God.

iv) The word must be attended by the power of God. At the point of delivery a prophetic word is not the property of the prophetic speaker, it belongs to God. Whatever the directive, warning, or encouragement, the responsibility for the power released through the words themselves to enact the changes God wants lies solely with the One who is actually the author of those words – God Himself. It is remarkable that God will trust men and women to be His mouthpiece, as there is such a margin for human error as we fumble the pass, drop the baton, or become side-tracked and distracted so easily. The call of Jonah is a wonderful example of God's commitment to display His power in human weakness. Unfortunately, in Jonah's case everything that could go wrong did go wrong. But we are getting ahead of ourselves!

A ship to Tarshish anyone?

3. On the Run

(Jonah 1:1-3)

"In the fifteenth year of Amaziah the son of Joash, king of Judah, Jeroboam the son of Joash, king of Israel, began to reign in Samaria, and he reigned forty-one years. And he did what was evil in the sight of the Lord. He did not depart from all the sins of Jeroboam the son of Nebat, which he made Israel to sin. He restored the border of Israel from Lebo-hamath as far as the Sea of the Arabah, according to the word of the Lord, the God of Israel, which He spoke by His servant Jonah the son of Amittai, the prophet, who was from Gath-hepher. For the Lord saw that the affliction of Israel was very bitter, for there was none left, bond or free, and there was none to help Israel. But the Lord had not said that He would blot out the name of Israel from under heaven, so He saved them by the hand of Jeroboam the son of Joash."

(2 Kings 14:23-27)

Apart from the book that bears his name, the only other reference to Jonah the prophet in Old Testament scripture is in this passage in 2 Kings 14. Although we refer to Jonah as a minor prophet (due to the brevity of the book, not the impact of his ministry) it is clear that even before He called him to Nineveh, God was speaking clearly through him to the nation of Israel. A prophet is someone who is commissioned to mediate God's timely word to a particular people in a particular situation at a particular time – a kind of bespoke word for those who most need to hear it. God's "now word" for the need of the hour. As far as the recipients are concerned there is no other word.

Jonah did not begin his prophetic career with the call to Nineveh. God rarely speaks such radical and costly words to someone unprepared or ill-equipped to receive them. Instead, He takes time to teach them to hear His voice in different contexts and for different reasons and seasons. There will be successes and failures, joys and sorrows, times of clarity and times of opacity, but all the while God is increasing the capacity of the prophet to hear, and speak, His word.

Good times

During the reign of King Jeroboam the second, the nation of Israel was enjoying a particularly prosperous and fruitful season, mainly to do with her geographical location as a gateway of economic trade between east and west. Friendly links between the nations of that area meant that there were open trade routes into Israel's borders and waters that had been lost during the reign of Solomon.

The increase of foreign visitors to Israel led to a shift in religious tolerance and soon, the people of God were engaging in idolatry of the most serious kind. However, unlike the prophets Amos and Hosea who were led by God to castigate the nation of Israel, Jonah was commissioned to preach only a positive message. Rather than telling Israel that her name would be erased, Jonah prophesied the opposite. Jonah loved preaching to the converted. He left "the dirty work" to others who were wired for this – Amos or Hosea.

Far from being a prophet of doom and destruction, Jonah was the good guy whose words were comforting and warm. We all like telling people exactly what they want to hear, and getting paid to do so if possible. Perhaps he was content to be the positive prophet whose role was to encourage and build up. Everyone likes to be liked. Maybe this suited Jonah fine. Honour and financial rewards may have enriched God's prophet as a reward for his encouraging, affirming ministry. We call this "Feathered Nest Syndrome". It's often time God broke up the nest.

With the call to Nineveh, everything was about to change.

The problem

God had planned a rescue package for Nineveh in the form of his prophet Jonah. If the plan was to succeed, it needed Jonah to be fully on board and ready to obey God every step of the way. To some degree, it was a simple request: Go to Nineveh and speak out against it. There were no complex timings and there was no need for a secret strategy to be executed with a newly recruited army in the dead of night.

Jonah was only to speak a few faithful words. Such ministry is radical, deeply unsettling, and potentially revolutionary for that people or nation.

The problem was, however, that Jonah was afraid of what would happen to him when he did this. This call was not the immense privilege he had come to expect of the office of prophet; it was a mission that would likely lead him to hostility, imprisonment or even worse, death.

God does not always make life comfortable. There will be times when, if we remember the naivety of our earnest prayer, "Use me Lord," repeated regularly in the early days of our walk with Him, we may wish we could backtrack and put some conditions on it! He takes us at our word. When we make ourselves available to Him, opportunities open up before us that will stretch our boundaries of understanding and expectation. This will be either exhilarating or exhausting, depending on the personal cost to us. For Jonah, the prospect of a visit to Nineveh was not a happy one. After perhaps little sober reflection he was ready to run in the opposite direction.

This reminds me of an event some years ago when my wife Ruth and I lived in Lancashire midway between Liverpool and Manchester. Driving onto the M6 motorway heading north, we spotted three hitchhikers on the slip road, hoping for a lift. Each one had a sign held in front of them bearing the name of their preferred destination. The first read "Glasgow," the second "Carlisle" and the third read "Anywhere but here"!

Resistance and intimidation

Prophets are sent to tell both the Church and the world what neither of them usually want to hear.

When God called Jonah to go to Nineveh it took very little time for Jonah to respond to Him, and that, not in a good way. No sooner had God spoken than Jonah set off to flee in the opposite direction, far away from His presence (verse 3).

Jonah was resisting the same God to whom he had once cheerfully submitted. The life of a prophet is characterised by closeness to the presence of the Lord. Jonah would have become familiar with the ease by which he could access the will of God through prophetic utterance. For Jonah, the presence of the Lord had once been a special privilege of the call upon his life. Now, however, Jonah was determined to turn away from that very same presence, by running as far away from it as possible. Any thought of partnership with God had been annihilated by the troublesome call to the city of Nineveh.

Jonah was intimidated by the threat of harm or evil. Reports of the brutality that took place in Nineveh would have certainly reached Jonah's ears. To hear of a race of people who would build pyramids of severed human heads outside the city walls of their enemies was reason enough make Jonah rigid with fear.

Knowing that God wanted to speak seriously to a people who did not even believe in Him, let alone worship Him, led Jonah to fear for his life if he set foot inside the city. His eyes would not be lifted confidently to heaven, but fixed on an earthly reality where prophets of God might lose their heads in hostile pagan lands.

Jonah had failed to acknowledge the faithfulness of God in his call. He gave way to fear, resisting the truth that whom God calls, He equips, protects and even hides. That God wanted Jonah to be his pivot person to shape the destiny of a wicked city reiterates His commitment to using men and women to fulfil His purposes.

Very often, we fail to understand the depths of loyalty God has to us when we submit to His will for our lives. He will not leave us, nor will He forsake us; His presence is something we can never run from, and can always rely on (Isaiah 42:16, Psalm 139:7-10).

Whether he liked it or not, one perhaps unwelcome consequence of this is that the presence of the Lord would be accompanying Jonah to Joppa and on the boat to Tarshish and beyond, but we will save our exploration of that reality for the chapters to come.

Jonah's responsibility

Although the original call was from the Lord, Jonah was personally required to carry the responsibility for conveying its implications to this lawless city. The partnership between Jonah and God was an essential ingredient in the success or failure of the mission. I have previously alluded to the fact that God, being God, was perfectly able to deal with Nineveh directly by wiping it off the face of the earth. But in His mercy, He used Jonah to both warn the people and invite, or at least provoke them, to repent.

God's word was to become a now word in a blithely indifferent and non-expectant place. It was to be spoken out by Jonah and heard by the people of Nineveh, who would then be obligated by the faith it triggered, to receive it and obey it. If they did not hear Jonah because he chose not to go, the city could not be saved. What an enormous responsibility for the prophet!

Nineveh was like the Third Reich of the ancient world. Its army would stop at nothing to crush any opposition to the expansion of its territory. Archaeological discoveries, now in the British Museum, depict battle scenes of the most graphic nature – Assyria's forces laying siege to whole cities with overwhelming forces armed with the most sophisticated weaponry and siege towers packed with ruthless "storm troopers". To be called by God to speak His words into a nation like this would be akin to today being called to do the same in some of the most brutal dictatorships in our world today. For Jonah, this was no well-deserved vacation. He would have considered that in all likelihood taking responsibility for this particular mission God had assigned to him, would have meant he was unlikely to return home. A one-way ticket to a living hell.

All of a sudden, the responsibility of being God's mouthpiece had lost its appeal. The American Old Testament scholar Walter Brueggemann broadens our concept of the importance of such faithful heralding when he defines this work in a striking way: "The task of prophetic ministry is to nurture, nourish and evoke a consciousness and perception alternative to the consciousness and perception of the dominant culture around us." God wanted Jonah to face Nineveh with an alternative bright reality, utterly different from the darkness to which they had become accustomed. In doing so, Jonah was likely to invite a hostile reaction as he swam against the filthy tide of degraded idolatry and its warped popular opinion.

Jonah's courage had failed him.

Why run?

If God is sovereign and chooses to have mercy on an individual, city or nation, we can guarantee that the story will end well, at least for many lives. When God commissioned Jonah, although the original message was less than merciful, Jonah would have known that God was doing this in order that the people of Nineveh would be given a second chance. So why did he run? I would like to conjecture some thoughts at this point.

1. Jonah was scared

I have already reasoned that Jonah understood the seriousness of God's call to Nineveh and that he might not return home. We also know he had enjoyed some years of celebrity status, living in the fruitful prosperity of the nation of Israel as a "good news prophet". Why would he want to leave such a receptive and willing audience? Why would he choose to put himself in extreme danger in an unfamiliar and hostile land? What would happen to him if he did?

How easy it is to allow fear to dominate our thinking! Faith requires us to trust God when we can't see the way ahead or have no answers as yet to our anxieties. When God calls us in a radical way, it may well mean that we are required to leap out of the cosy predictability of our comfort zone into the danger of the largely unknown. The places we are sometimes called to may well be unfamiliar and prove to be hostile. Will we allow fear to overthrow the truth that God is always faithful to supply our every need? (Philippians 4:19)

2. Jonah thought his words would fail

After years of being established as a true prophet of God, Jonah was comfortable with his reputation and positive identity. People listened to him. When he spoke, his hearers would know that God was speaking. Now Jonah was faced with a conundrum: how would the people of Nineveh receive him? To them, he was an Israelite imposter, speaking words from an alien foreign God with whom they did not align themselves. What if they called him a false prophet? What if they ridiculed him, stoned him, or wanted to torture him?

When we value our calling more than the One who has called us, we begin to feel insecure when there is a threat to our identity. Sometimes, God will take us outside of our familiar places of operation, allowing us to encounter the uncomfortable in order that we will not forget that whatever gift has been given to us, we do not own it. It is on loan to us. Scripture says all that is good and perfect belongs to God (James 1:17), so we should never fear failure if we are following the Lord and exercising His gifts with integrity and humility, even if we cannot foresee what the results will be.

3. Jonah was racially prejudiced

It is impossible to know how often, if at all, Jonah travelled to foreign lands and peoples prior to his call to Nineveh. The only other prophetic activity we read about in which he was involved is in the 2 Kings passage. So we can only speculate on how he felt about the call to go to a place outside of Israel. Thankfully, God was not, and is not, a tribal deity and personal "club mascot" reserved for only a few. Even when, in the Old Testament accounts, He called Himself the God of Israel and was clear that they were His chosen people, God reached out time and time again to people of other tribes and tongues. The depravity of Nineveh was something He could bear no longer. He longed to offer them an opportunity to experience the revelation of His truth and their subsequent repentance.

Whatever God felt, Jonah was required to feel that too. Perhaps he did not understand the compassion of God for the lost in the way he should have done? But then, how moved are we by the misery and plight of strangers?

4. Jonah did not care enough

The gospel accounts often tell us that before Jesus healed a man, woman or child, he was "moved with compassion" (Matthew 14:14). The original word for "compassion" in Greek, is related to our word "spleen" – it describes a "gut-level love" that we feel in our viscera. What moves God to act? What initiated His call to Jonah? Compassion for the city of Nineveh.

For Jonah to obey the call, he had to feel what God felt. Perhaps his response to flee was partly to do with his inability to empathise with God's heart. Prophets can be tricky to relate to at times because they feel the heartbeat of God for situations and people. It can be a heavy burden at times. A prophecy spoken out with costly accuracy, faithfulness and integrity will carry compassion and grace with it, even if it is a serious warning. This is simply because God is always motivated by love before He is motivated by judgement. Mercy, the Bible tells us, triumphs over judgement (James 2:13).

Jonah was required to demonstrate "the power of one", standing alone in the middle of a city God loved. In doing that, he was required to reach out in faith and be willing to let the same flow of love God displays to pass through his heart and through his lips. Was he ready to do that? Are you?

The compassion of God for today

There are aspects of life in modern Great Britain and the wider western nations, that are just as offensive to God as the sins of Nineveh. God has called His Church to be an instrument in His hand to dismantle the decay and erect something beautiful in its place. He wants His word to be switched on, broadcast persuasively, and to invade the darkness for His light to shine.

There is a lack of hope in so many, but there is no such thing as a hopeless believer (Ephesians 2:11-13; 1 Thessalonians 1:3). A "hopeless believer" is a contradiction in terms. People are increasingly tired of lies and spin. They ache for an encounter with love and truth, even if they never articulate this publicly. They also recognise truth and feel the power of it when they suddenly encounter it. God's truth is captivating. The compassion of Christ goes out with it, like a healing balm to soothe the sick soul. And He is looking for those who will lean into His heartbeat, hearing the word of truth, and seeing how it resonates for His lost world, even among it's most far off and hardened people. Miracles of transformation are possible.

With God, there is no room for prejudice of any kind. He is not partial to saving particular people groups or a particular race. How easy it is to absorb the same aggressive and suspicious attitudes we imbibe from the media! Reports of events around the world filter into our consciousness, leading us to form negative opinions about our neighbour, whom the Bible tells us to love as we love ourselves (Matthew 19:19). Even if we can't love them as our friends, we are still commanded by Jesus to love them as our enemies (Matthew 5:43-48).

What do we do when we feel superior or even suspicious toward the street sweeper, the shop assistant or the parking attendant? How do we learn to hear and feel the compassion of God for the prostitute, the pimp and the paedophile? Do we have a bias against the poor and for the rich? Or do we criticise those who we feel have "more money than sense?" What should our response be to the tensions between the Israelis and the Palestinians? Closer to home, how do we feel when the church down our road is more lively, friendly and highly motivated than our own church? Do we feel the pangs of jealousy or are we genuinely delighted that God is working there?

The call of Jonah should be a challenge to us. This book is an invitation to examine whether we would, along with Jonah, have run away from God's call or embraced it fully in faith. Even though we have only looked so far at the first four verses of chapter 1, the text is rich with meaning and offers this sober challenge:

Will we willingly partner with God to be His mouthpiece to a messed up world, or will we look for the next boat to Tarshish?

Jonah's flight

If everything had gone immediately to plan, Jonah would have been travelling east to Nineveh. Instead, he ran as fast as his little legs could carry him to the coastal city of Joppa in order to board a boat to Tarshish. He was about to find out that, try as he might, he could never escape from God and he could not escape from the man and messenger God had called him to be. I want to resist the temptation to explain prematurely exactly why Jonah did this. After all, if you had never read the Jonah narrative before, you would have to wait until chapter 4 and verse 2 before everything was revealed. Jonah wasn't sacked by God due to his unworthy motives, he simply quit his job and set sail in the opposite direction.

Warning! Tarshish is attractive

In real life, there is always a ship to Tarshish! Some call it, "The grass is always greener" syndrome. It echoes the sentiment of the hitchhiker on the M6 ramp who preferred to go "anywhere but here" rather than staying in his hometown.

When the going gets tough we feel like we want to escape. When God has entrusted us with so many resources, He requires us to grow. Karen Kaiser Clark states, "Life is change. Growth is optional. Choose carefully." Simply changing our place of residence or current job, because we "fancy a change" does not guarantee our growth.

When Jonah fled, he was looking to change his geography, but not his heart. It is vital we stay open to the guidance of God as we seek to grow. He always plans greater things for us than we could ever plan for ourselves. It may not always be pleasant, at least initially, but it will always be good. We simply have to wait and see.

Tarshish was situated in the southern part of Spain at the western end of the Mediterranean Sea. As far as Jonah was concerned, it was the end of the world as far as he knew it. Some of us want to get far away, to the end of our world, wherever that may be, but we need to recognise that this may not be God's best for us. Eugene Peterson explains the hidden agenda behind this kind of decision:

"In Tarshish we can have a religious career without having to deal with God."

God may have called you to stay where you are. He may want to use you in amazing ways, but you may not have seen this as yet. Life can be boring, bland and banal at times. We picture ourselves in a romantic place, full of new and pleasant surprises, without a care in the world, unfettered by the demands of people and projects, free to be who we want to be. But who we want to be may not be who God wants us to be, because God knows us better than we know ourselves.

Are you running away, or are you prepared to stay on course with God?

For Jonah, Nineveh was a dangerous place, but it was much less dangerous than where that boat to Tarshish would be taking him. There, he would be outside of God's best for his life. But he had to find that out for himself. It comes down to this: either *we* die or *Nineveh* dies. But Jonah, quite literally, "Couldn't give a damn".

And that is precisely the problem.

4. The Wake Up Call

(Jonah 1:3-9)

The call of God to Jonah was crystal clear:

"Arise, go to Nineveh, that great city, and call out against it, for their evil has come up before me." (1:2)

In quick response, Jonah had made the life-changing decision to run in totally the opposite direction from the city, and far away from the call of God. Life in Tarshish promised peace, tranquillity, comfort and anonymity. The opposite was true of life in Nineveh, a city in the east that offered no benefit to such a prophet accustomed to the perks of the role of Israel's "in-house" messenger of God, who were a captive and sympathetic audience. There, Jonah was fêted and honoured; in Nineveh he was likely to be ignored, mocked and at worst, annihilated.

Jonah had heard the call and rejected it. He had entered into an alternative world of fantasy: a world in which he could justify his position as the messenger who could pick and choose the missions given to him by God, based on their appeal and likely outcome.

Things can only get better

Here is the irony. The journey to Tarshish, a place that promised so much relief, ease and freedom, was to become a voyage of unrest, danger and loneliness, as Jonah encountered the reality of life outside God's will. Running away from the call to Nineveh would expose Jonah to the very dangers he wanted to avoid. God was about to make things so much worse before they could get better.

God speaks intentionally through prophetic men and women into the destiny of an individual, church, city or nation. His words are heavy with significance and rich with meaning. He will not waste words, nor will He make mistakes or change His mind (Numbers 23:19).

The testimony of the Jonah narrative bears witness to the commitment of God to fulfil His word no matter what the cost. He had chosen Jonah as His human agent to facilitate this, and there would be no place for the prophet to hide. Nor would Jonah be at peace until he chose to walk into the destiny laid out for him. He was about to be awakened by an alarm call from heaven, roused from his sleep by God who Himself never slumbers or sleeps.

Alarm calls are rarely welcome. They shatter our comfort, invade our dreams and pull us back into reality. When God stuns us with a wake-up alarm, it is usually to alert us to the dangers we are in that we may know nothing about. Life may feel comfortable and easy, yet we are oblivious to how far we have travelled from His purposes for us. He may choose to shatter our comforts for a season in order that we can be realigned to the deepest joys of life in the centre of His will.

At the point when Jonah decided to run away, events were set in motion that were to expose the prophet to the dire consequences of his choice. The following three disturbing stages opened up during his flight.

Jonah's evasion

"But Jonah rose to flee to Tarshish from the presence of the Lord. He went down to Joppa and found a ship going to Tarshish. So he paid the fare and went on board, to go with them to Tarshish, away from the presence of the Lord" (verse 3).

It looked like Jonah was perfectly safe. He had successfully executed his bid for freedom and had encountered no angry lightning bolts of judgement from heaven in the process. He had got away with it! God did nothing; no further voices were heard and Jonah could embark on his exciting new life in the sun. It would take only a few days to get to Joppa (modern day Jaffa) from where he would catch the next available ship to Tarshish, which was probably in the region of today's southern Spain.

The onerous task of prophesying to Nineveh was becoming a distant memory and all was well in Jonah's world. He was about to board a ship to take him far, far away through sparkling, turquoise waters to a land of new opportunity and promise. Jonah himself had carved out this alternative destiny; and due to the fact that God had not struck him down on the spot, he was now at peace again. God had kindly released him from all obligations and obviously understood his dilemma. In reality, nothing could have been further from the truth.

So what made it feel so easy?

1. The circumstances were just right

Initially, Jonah experienced ideal sailing conditions as he set sail for Tarshish. Not only that, but as soon as he arrived in the busy port of Joppa at the end of the first leg of his journey, he saw that a ship was just about to set sail going to that very same destination across the Mediterranean. What a remarkable co-incidence! It was as if circumstances had conspired in his favour and God was smiling on him. What a relief! God would surely carve out a more attractive alternative destiny for his burned-out pastor-preacher, one more in keeping with his temperament and positive outlook.

Not only does Tarshish represent an alluring image for the weary pastor in need of rest from God's call, but the account of the favourable conditions prior to Jonah getting there could mislead any of us to believe that too. It's often the case that when things are going well in our lives, we are certain we must be in the will of God. God is in His heaven, and everything is alright with the world. We conclude God must be in it, including all the details.

However, it does not always happen this way. The truth is, paradoxically, that when we are on the run from God, very great conveniences often appear to facilitate the flight. But appearances can be misleading. We are led into a false sense of security that God understands it all and will accommodate our choices and change His mind about His destiny for us. Be warned, though, that although God promises life in all its fullness, He rarely makes our journey to that desirable outcome as comfortable as we anticipated.

God requires faithfulness to His call, through times of joy and times of hardship, providing all we need to follow it on a day by day basis. When the lure of a better looking job, increased salary, nicer town or livelier church causes us to turn our faces away from the clear call of God for our lives, we need to remain focussed and faithful in case unusual occurrences mislead us. Otherwise we will sail directly into the kind of divine "wake-up" call that was about to happen to Jonah.

2. Jonah was offered a safe passage

The nation of Israel was not renowned for its sea-faring adventures. It was a place through which other nations would pass on busy and profitable trade routes both east and west, so there was no requirement for the Israelites to venture onto the high seas. Jonah would therefore be boarding a Phoenician ship from a port in Philistine territory – a place where the Jews had historically battled and defeated their enemies and where hostility still bubbled ominously beneath the surface. Jonah is passing through dangerous territory, and soon to join a happy crew of pagans who would regret offering sea-passage to this unusual stranger.

However, the sailors were quite happy to have Jonah on board, caring very little about past events and old grudges. Here were old enemies who had become new friends and Jonah must have marvelled at the ease of his get-away journey thus far. The ship was ready to sail and the Lord was leading him to a new place. Perhaps he considered that he was about to be called to a new mission field in Tarshish, a place that knew nothing of the God of Israel and perhaps his former mistake could be redeemed by the potential good that could come of it.

Friendly people are not always sent from God. To Jonah, the amiable sailors represented another indication that confirmed that God was making his journey to Tarshish as smooth as possible. Surely if he was outside of God's plans, the sailors would have been hostile, and the passenger list full? The truth was not that simple.

In reality, we can be surrounded by dangerous secular-minded people who seem to enjoy our company and with whom we are popular and friendly, but these are the very people who could side-track us away from the Lord, without proper vigilance. Perhaps you are in a wrong relationship with an attractive and vibrant non-believer who does not share your passion for Christ. It could be that you have charming work colleagues who, after hours, invite you to engage in activities that compromise your conscience and integrity. Have you enrolled on a study programme that constantly assaults your belief system, eroding your biblical worldview and Christian convictions day by day? Maybe you have rejected your old church in favour of one that promises a trendy new style of expression, but devalues the importance of authentic biblical theology.

We can become blinded by the allure of new ventures, new relationships, seductive ideas, a change of job, church or house. There is an appeal in the freshness of unchartered waters and the offer of a safe passage out of the old and into the new. "I believe God is in this, and is leading me to leave here and experience something new, something different in what lies ahead", he might have reflected. The truth is, Jonah was right. But not in the way he anticipated.

3. Jonah paid the necessary fare

By handing over a large sum of money to pay for his voyage, Jonah in effect seals his decision. His resources are being invested not in God's mission, but in his own chosen alternative adventure of a lifetime. Jonah was not just going to the next port, he was leaving for good, and was prepared to pay any price and invest his life savings to get as far away from God as possible. In effect, he was prepared to pay good money to indulge his high-handed sin.

The Bible teaches us that the love of money is the root of every kind of evil (1 Timothy 6:10). Not only can it become an obsession as we seek to get rich quick, but it can be used to facilitate our own selfish desires.

Many Christians, who see their own money as an entitlement, will use it to fuel lifestyles counter to the ways of God, sinking deeper and deeper into addictions and promiscuity. What begins as an innocuous dabble in some shallow and harmless waters for some, will soon become a full-blown storm at sea, as the consequences of their wilful choice to compromise become much more serious. No matter how much money Jonah spent to ensure his safe passage to Tarshish, it would not be anywhere near as costly as the experience that was about to hit him in the middle of the sea.

Are you on the run from God?

Can you feel Him breathing down your neck in His pursuit of you? Initially, it is entirely possible to run away from God, as He is not an oppressive despot who keeps us permanently in chains. He wants us to partner with Him through a relationship of love, not a regime of fear, so He will allow us to run, watching our flight with ever deepening sadness. But none of us should indulge the illusions that the Lord will "rubber stamp" our choices, and that will be the end of it. He loves us too much to let us get away with it. He loves Nineveh too much to leave the matter there. "Fleeing the presence..." (verse 3) often proves to be the biggest mistake of our lives.

There are times in life when we come to a crossroads where two ways meet and we have a choice as to which road we take. Unfortunately, we can sometimes make the wrong choice and as we begin to walk boldly ahead, we start to feel an unease that had not been there before. Autonomous living, where we decide for ourselves what is best for our life, will never offer the peace and freedom it promises. We will only know the deepest peace once we relinquish our selfishness and submit to the One who knows what is best for us.

We do this by continually assessing whether we have become independent from God's presence or not. To ask the question, "Where is God in this?" is precisely the opposite from anything Jonah asked up to this point in the narrative. He had paid the necessary fare for the journey to Tarshish but he failed to ask where God was in this. Nothing scary had happened so far, so He concluded that nothing ever would. He had become independent of all connection to heaven, and, as in Genesis 3, had pushed away the truth of the words God had originally spoken to him.

Did God really say...?

It is this same independence and arrogance that has often kept the 21st century Church in a state of compromise and confusion. We have a "pick and mix" philosophy in matters of faith and theology and all too often the Church in this country has failed to adhere to the eternal truths of Scripture as unchanging and irrevocable, seeking to bend and accommodate them to current philosophy and thinking. But to marry "the spirit of the age" is to become a widow in the next one.

In a place of desert and deprivation, severely tempted by Satan, Jesus was unwavering in His commitment to the truth of the Word of God. Three times he spoke out, "It is written" as a block to the deception of the enemy who sought to overthrow His calling and divert His destiny. Jesus was offered the kingdom without the Cross. In His wisdom, vigilance and faith, He set His face to hold the line on God's truth. This is to characterise our choices also.

We must be people who remain steadfast and refuse to be tossed around by the pressures of the world or the latest fashion or whim that seeks to keep us from our destiny and calling. Jesus has paid the ultimate price. Will we?

4. Jonah had a tremendous sense of wellbeing

Once he had boarded the ship, Jonah was free to bask in the pleasure of life at sea. The crisis was over. The sun warmed his back, the gulls squawked overhead, the sea breeze blew his hair, the waves lapped, and the gentle spray of the sea splashed his face. The sailors would maybe tell him stories of their sea-faring adventures amid howls of laughter and gasps of surprise, and he would have convinced himself, perhaps, that no one outside of God's will would ever experience such kindness and favour. God *must* be pleased with him. Ahead of him lay a new life away from all that Nineveh nonsense. Why go to the barrenness of Nineveh when you can sail the Mediterranean in fine company like this?

How could it be so wrong when it feels so right?

For Jonah, his feelings of wellbeing masked the truth that there was nothing right about the choice he had made at all. The writer of the Jonah account tells us that four times Jonah "went down" - to Joppa, to the portside, to the hold of the ship, and even into a deep sleep (1:3-5). In other words, everything is going downhill for him, and things are about to get a whole lot worse.

A word of warning: feelings are rarely the indicator that we are in God's will. A sense of wellbeing can indeed accompany being in the right place with God, but emotions are not the arbiter of whether we are in God's will or not. Just because I may feel something is right, does not mean that it is. Remember to discern so that you are not in any danger of being deceived badly.

Jonah's exposure

Jonah's excitement and *joie de vivre* was very short lived as, in no time, God caught up with him. Jonah was about to be exposed.

"But the Lord hurled a great wind upon the sea, and there was a mighty tempest on the sea, so that the ship threatened to break up." (1:4)

The wind and storm were so strong that the ship threatened to break up. The sailors began to throw cargo overboard, crying out to their own gods to save them. Jonah had gone down below deck to sleep and was oblivious to the chaos around him. In the cool shade of the hold, Jonah had snuggled down and fallen into a peaceful oblivion where all was right with his world. He had lost touch with God, idly dreaming and out of touch with reality.

How easy it is to see Jonah as a picture of how many see the Church today: in some kind of fantasy world, a safe religious cocoon, out of touch with the reality of God's call, oblivious and uncaring about the chaos of the world around them, and unable to be woken up by the cries of the terrified and the desperate.

The storms that rage

Terrific storms have been brewing all around our world for over a century. The historical TV series, *The People's Century*, made some years ago, depicted the atrocities committed by dictators with a frightening lust for power. Stalin, Pol Pot, Idi Amin, Mussolini, Milosevic, Hitler, Mao and the Ayatollah Khomeini have, amongst others, unleashed storms of wickedness that have threatened to break up the very fabric of human existence.

What is the response of God's people, the Church, to such evil? When people choose to live in autonomous independence, crushing the innocent and destroying nations, what is our call?

Tragically, the Church has all too often "done a Jonah" and run away, to hide and retreat until the storm safely passes. We have absorbed the same self-will and dependence on human reason as the world that ridicules God. We submit to it's reductionism and wilful intent to decide what is true and what is not by human reason alone, denying God the opportunity to use us to bring divine revelation from God's Word and supernatural change for the better.

God is faithful to the world He has made, but His Church is so often asleep amid the storms that rage around it.

Whilst societies fragment and crack under the pressure of evil forces, we hide in the hold and dream of revival, but refuse to do anything that would prepare for a divine visitation in power.

It is time to wake up!

Awake or asleep?

When you are asleep certain things are true of you that are not true of a person who is fully awake. The same is true of the Church today. As an organization, it tends to have people within it whose understanding of current affairs derives from their close attention to the world's media, accurate theological perspective on most things, cultural relevance and responsiveness to a hurting world. There is a genuine belief among many that the Church in our nation is functioning exactly as it should be.

Nothing could be further from the truth.

To outsiders the Church is often seen as irrelevant, powerless and, at times, downright silly. Just as a sleeping person may do strange and irritating things while asleep such as snoring, shouting out, muttering gibberish or dribbling saliva, the Church can be oblivious to how odd it can appear to someone looking in. People shake their heads and wonder what planet we are on, and how out of touch we are. We are often oblivious to reality and out of touch even with the living God. It is surely time for us to awaken and become effective again!

Jonah fell fast asleep at the wrong time and in the wrong place. God had a special mission for him to perform. He should not have been asleep in the hold of a ship sailing to Tarshish! This false peace and untroubled slumber we know cannot last for long, and there will soon be a moment when Jonah will encounter His God again and be faced with a choice as to whether he will reverse his downhill slide, or not.

There would be no revival in Tarshish for Jonah, if God has sent him to Nineveh! The promise of blessing in this alternative land to the west was a figment of Jonah's own imagination. God had not promised Jonah a thing regarding Tarshish, at least not at this time. He wanted him to go to Nineveh and announce God's warning, then do something signal as a result of Jonah's obedience, in order to facilitate Nineveh's recovery. Tarshish was not on God's agenda.

We will not see our own longed-for revival by imagining then implementing our own plans and schedules. God knows what He wants. Going through the motions of how things used to be will never cut it in the 21st century. Everyone who is backsliding downhill in rebellion to God's ways and call upon their lives is foolishly killing time when God has called us all to redeem the time.

What will it take to wake us up again?

Throughout history God has shaken men and women who are hungry for change into a renewed longing and experience of the atmosphere of revival. Back in the 18th century, Britain was in at least as bad a state as it is in the 21st century, possibly far worse. In London gin houses and opium dens, people would feed their addictions and advertised that customers could, "Get drunk for a penny, dead drunk for tuppence." Alcoholism was rife and vast numbers of the population were involved in binge drinking. There was violent crime in the streets, cities were unsafe after dark, the churches were dead or dying, and the clergy spoke irrelevant drivel to their dwindling congregations. Feelings of hopelessness and loneliness permeated the lives of millions of people.

Amid this decadence and desperation, God decided to awaken His Church. Tucked away in Oxford University were young men, undergraduates training for the Anglican ministry, men like John and Charles Wesley along with the phenomenal son of a Gloucester inn-keeper, George Whitfield, all of whom were beginning to feel spiritually stirred. They became conscientious about how to please God and how to serve others, leading such disciplined spiritual lives that it earned them the pejorative nickname "Methodists", from their hostile peers. God got hold of these young men, all aged between seventeen to twenty years, joining together in what they called "The Holy Club" to pray, read stirring Christian books and urge one another to seek God - much like the way God would soon get hold of Jonah in the coming verses.

What happened in the next 50 years all over Britain and in the colonies of America during the 18th century came to be called "The Great Awakening", a movement that shook both sides of the Atlantic Ocean. I want to encourage you to read the accounts of it, as it will amaze and utterly stun you awake from any slumber you may presently still be in. Only a wide-awake church can awaken a sleeping world.

It's time to wake up!

5. Jonah Wakes Up

(Jonah 1:3-9)

The prophetic message of the book of Jonah declares the enduring truth of the commitment of God to His people. As the narrative unfolds, we continue to be profoundly affected by the grace of God to the prophet Jonah, His heart for the city of Nineveh and the lengths to which He will go to connect the two.

Jonah, dog-tired from his flight westwards to Joppa, most likely on foot, went below deck and fell into a deep, undisturbed and stupefied sleep. As Jonah sleeps, God prepares to shake his world. The storm that shatters the peace of Jonah's unreality echoes down the centuries – as countless men and women testify to similar encounters. In his epistle to the Ephesian church, the apostle Paul encourages the Christians to be wide awake to the surrounding pagan culture and its vices:

"Awake, O sleeper, and arise from the dead and Christ will shine on you." (Ephesians 5:14)

Rocking the boat

Jonah was so deeply asleep that God had to send a storm of extraordinary magnitude to wake him up. The different translations of the Bible in Jonah 1:4 describe how the Lord, "hurled a great wind upon the sea..." (ESV), "sent out a great wind on the sea" (NKJV), "...a huge storm at sea, the waves towering." (The Message), indicating a sudden violent end to Jonah's peaceful and seemingly favourable flight from God.

This working ship, sailing inconspicuously through familiar and predictable waters was about to be tossed around by the hand of God. Jonah had tried to hide but God knew where he was, and He was about to identify his true significance and expose him in the most terrifying way.

We could ask ourselves why God would bother going to all this trouble to pick out Jonah once more. Why not allow him to simply slip away? Could He not just look elsewhere among His other chosen and called prophets for someone more reliable and less fickle?

The answer lies in God's commitment to finishing what He has started. The call to Jonah was still active, still relevant and still important. God had not finished with Jonah, even though Jonah had, at this point, finished with God by rejecting his mission to Nineveh. God did not want anyone else to do the job; He had chosen His man and would see to it that the relationship was restored and the mission re-booted.

How often we discount ourselves from a radical life with God because we feel either unworthy of His call and struggle to obey it, or we believe the lie that there is someone better suited to the task. We hide away in our weakness and self-doubt, not understanding that God will finish what He has started in us and He will creatively lead us back into right relationship with Himself by waking us up to the truth that He wants *us* and nobody else. Sometimes He will send a storm and sometimes a whispered word, but He will always find us, wherever we are. Be encouraged that God does not give up as easily as we ourselves sometimes do.

Jonah's awakening

The wake up call was set in motion as two elements conspired to turn the situation around for the better. To the reader of the account in Jonah 1:4-9 it appears that things are getting worse for the prophet. But in reality, these two key strategies of God proved to be effective in Jonah's awakening, turning things around for the better. The first is *the call of the wild* and the second *the call of the world*.

The unpredictability of such a wild and terrifying storm at sea meant that it literally was a case of "all hands on deck" in order to prevent the sinking of the ship and loss of life. But while the sailors battled to stay afloat, Jonah slept on, until the captain himself went down to the hold and woke Jonah with some strong strident words,

"What do you mean, you sleeper? Arise, call out to your god! Perhaps the god will give a thought to us, that we may not perish." (1:6)

Today, we are discovering an uncannily similar parallel to this. Tough times and a tough world have conspired to give God's prophetic body, the Church, a good shaking. Both wild nature and troubled human society are ringing like alarm bells in the ears of the body of Christ and by God's grace we can awaken once again to the calling and mandate we have been given to heal a messed-up world with God's gospel.

1. The call of the wild

God, who is in control of nature, can command it to move however and whenever He wants. We recall how the disciples marvelled at Jesus' command of the elements when he calmed the boiling sea of Galilee,

"Who then is this, that even the wind and the sea obey him?" (Mark 4:41)

Here, the Lord had whipped up a violent storm, shattering the tranquillity of the Mediterranean Sea and sending the sailors into dread and panic. The waves were rolling over the sides of the ship, the sails were ripped and shredded, everything on deck was sliding around and the threat of drowning came ever closer. Cargo was hauled up and tossed into the sea in an attempt to stabilize and lighten the load. Steering the ship safely to port was top priority from now on and the desperate cries of the sailors rang out as they appealed to their own gods for the preservation of their brine-soaked lives.

Where was Jonah?

While there was pandemonium above deck, the prophet of God remained in a comatozed state in the hold, snoozing peacefully without a care in the world. He could not hear the cries and he could not feel the fear. Neither was he aware of his responsibility for both the real reason for the storm, nor how instrumental he could be in its cessation. Similar to Jesus, but without the same power, Jonah had the capacity to "speak" into the storm "Peace, be still" once he awoke to the call of God once again. But his sullen silence was the very thing that had led to this crisis, whilst an even greater storm was brewing for Nineveh.

God's message to the Church

God is speaking to His Church in the same way today. Our world is in need of holy calm, and the body of Christ is the instrument

even awake. There are unbelievers across the world that, in the same way, are becoming afraid of the God of heaven and earth who shakes nations and holds creation in the palm of His hand. The gods of this world are nothing compared to Him. Just as the sailors could not be saved by pleading with their pagan deities, the whole earth can only be restored by the One who made it, and the One who died to save it. Dead gods can offer no help at all. The living God can.

This is the call of the wild. It is designed to shatter our misconceptions about ourselves. When it becomes more difficult for the Church to suffer than to change, we will change. Jonah believed he was no longer useful so he went to sleep, but God woke him up with a storm to convince him of his true value.

We need to believe the truth that our day is not over, and respond by standing firm against the lies of the enemy. Never let anyone tell you the lie that, as God's people,

- You have had your day and are no longer useful
- Your gifts are insufficient and your God is not powerful
- You have nothing to say and nothing to contribute to this world
- Your past failures disqualify you from being God's messenger
- You are better off lying low, for one day it will all simply go away

Each one of these statements should be reversed to read the opposite. God is telling you to wake up. He has not given up on you and He never will. You have a destiny with Him that will simply never go away. The right time is now.

2. The call of the world
The Church has lost its identity in a world increasingly fascinated by spirituality. People with no formal religious belief are

becoming religious about the supernatural world and hungry for transcendence and greater reality.

In the 1990s there was a seismic shift in focus away from the pursuit of individual wealth that characterized the 80s, and onto spiritual things in order to find a deeper meaning to life. The outpouring of national grief at the sudden death of Princess Diana in August 1997 was tangibly spiritual in its expression. We had taken her to our heart and now we worshipped at her shrine. The pavements strewn with heaped bouquets of flowers along with the weeping multitudes of mourners on the streets, all bore witness to the deep longing for a saviour, believing that this iconic saviour was dead. Very few knew that a true and living Saviour was available for them.

With the advent of the attacks on the World Trade Center in September 2001 we were faced with fear on a global scale. People looked death in the face and cried out for hope, but hope was in short supply.

Research conducted among un-churched young people around this time revealed that they longed for the same things found in the New Testament Church, namely:

• *A longing to be loved.* When we love one another it is an overflow of God's love in Christ expressed at Calvary. As Christians, we experience God's love on a daily basis. How desperate our world is for the same expression of love, and a personal experience of it.

• *A longing for relationships.* Christ died to reconcile us to God, each other, and even to God's world, so that we could live in authentic and mutually beneficial relationship. How many people need to hear this simple truth. God's *shalom* has arrived with Jesus.

- *A longing to experience meaningful community.* The Church is the family of God; a place you can share your life with others and be profoundly changed for the better by God's word and Holy Spirit. How important it is for our world to know that church is a safe and valuable place to be. Wherever the Church is vibrant and healthy, there is no experience on earth that is quite like it.

When these same young people were asked what they would give to find these things if they were available, the answer was "Everything!"

In his book on the New Age, the late Christian writer and broadcaster Rob Frost wrote:

"To be frank, I am deeply disillusioned with what the Church is offering Sunday by Sunday. There is a deadness in ritual, a dryness in the formality and a growing irrelevance in the institution."

In his insightful book *Invading Secular Space*, Christian researcher Martin Robinson observed that a common perception of the Church was that it is "...narrow-minded, bigoted, lacking humour, devoid of imagination, incapable of understanding the real world, and occupying a sub-culture normal people wouldn't want to occupy." (p69)

Yet here are people crying for love, relationships and community. What will they find when they dare to cross the doorway of the Church? Will they even catch a glimpse of the things they hope for? The Jonah complex is all too common. No wonder people are staying away from our churches in the millions.

Prodded with questions

As Jonah came out of his deep sleep, the cries of the sailors would have resounded in his ears like the chimes of Big Ben in the late evening:

"How can you sleep?"

"Who are you?"

"Who is your God?"

"Why don't you ask Him to save you?"

"What have you done?"

"What should we do?"

The cumulative thrust of such urgent questions, after the casting of lots, is an echo of God's questions to His Church today. God is prodding us awake also. It may appear as a rude awakening, but it could issue in some kind of spiritual resurrection! He wants us to rediscover our identity, get up and take responsibility once again for much needed change and renewed compassion. We can no longer get away with blaming the previous generation, or the drug culture, or the Age of Aquarius, or secular humanism. Let's blame ourselves.

The simple yet profound truth is we have mislaid our calling and lost our identity in the whole shameful process, so that the world is astonished and incredulous in response to our indifference and avoidance.

Jonah's answer

Eventually, Jonah spoke up and admitted who he really was.

"And he said to them, 'I am a Hebrew, and I fear the Lord, the God of heaven, who made the sea and the dry land.'" (1:9)

This is a short sentence pregnant with significance. Jonah has acknowledged he is connected to Yahweh, the one true God. In the same way, it is the role of a prophetic Church to tell the world who is the authentic and only God; Father, Son and Holy Spirit. Notice that Jonah not only tells the sailors God's *name* but also His *nature*. He is the One who made the sea and dry land. So too, as we convey the truth of whom God is today, we must speak of His nature as creator of all things, one of the realities most regularly denied and disputed in our time. But if God didn't create the world, then he doesn't own the world – and that includes its people. There is no separate god of the river, rock, tree, wind or ocean. He is in all and He is all, the omnipresent, omniscient and omni-competent One. The rightful Owner of all things, including ourselves.

If God hasn't given us a reliable account of the origin of space, time, matter, earth, seas, dry land, water, plants, stars, sun and moon in Genesis 1, then what account can we turn to? If Genesis 1 is misleading, then how can we trust the rest of the Bible? "In the beginning God created the heavens and the earth…" is the foundational statement of the Bible, and the starting point for any credible all-embracing worldview that purports to answer all the most important questions in life including, *Who are we? What are we? How did we get here? What's gone wrong with us? How can it be put right? How long have we got?* All of the most reliable answers to these questions are found in the first few chapters of Genesis and expanded in the rest of the Bible. It's answers are the foundation and most cogent explanation of the only coherent life and worldview that makes total sense of everything, because the God who cannot lie has told us Total Truth, or "capital 'T' truth", in His Word, as the late Christian apologist Francis Schaeffer called it.

This reality was central to Jonah's first preaching to those pagan sailors, and it is also essential truth for our world today.

People of passion

The media frequently portrays Christians as well-meaning, bumbling, absent-minded, slightly overweight, giggly wimps with a secret weakness for sherry and cream cakes. That is indeed the view of students at Newcastle University who conducted a survey whose results showed they considered Christians to be "less free, less sexually fulfilled, more boring, more unfashionable, more isolated, psychologically weaker, less happy, less friendly and less realistic" than their non-Christian counterparts.

In the Jonah narrative, even the pagan sailors displayed more passion to avert Gods anger than Jonah himself did. They voice their hopes for a better life by saying to one another, "Perhaps the god will give a thought to us, that we may not perish." (1:6b)

Sometimes, the earnest interest and curiosity of those who don't know God, with their often relentless search for truth, hard work and self-discipline, challenges our own lack in those areas.

The Church needs to become a people of passion once again.

The challenge to us from the book of Jonah should call us to our knees in humility and repentance. We witness the devotion of men and women of other faiths across our nation and we have ignored the spotlight it shines on our own lack of discipline. Why do we not pray as much? Why is our faith so flabby? Why have we allowed our Christian heritage to be overwhelmed by other systems of belief at whose heart there is no self-existent and eternal God of love?

I sometimes drive through the East End of London and pass a large mosque on Fridays just as the men are pouring out after prayers, often forming a large crowd fifteen men deep on the pavement! It always prompts the question in my mind, "Where can we find so many men at a prayer meeting in our churches?" God wants His people to be people of devotion and passion without compromise. Living the Christian life requires us to reject the fantasy world of the hold of a ship where we dream dreams of ease and pleasure. We must wake up, climb up on deck and face the elements, ready to live or die for the call of the One we profess to worship.

It's YOU!

When Jonah woke up, he knew there was no more hiding, no more running. He had admitted his identity and told the sailors the name and nature of the God he worshipped. God was getting him ready for a new encounter with Himself because the people of Nineveh were waiting.

Who is waiting on you to move into your destiny and when will you make yourself available to God for it?

God calls people in myriads of ways and at countless different stages in their lives.

• Moses was called at eighty years of age to deliver 3 million Hebrew slaves from 400 years of captivity after he had killed an Egyptian and run for his life for forty years
• Esther became the main attraction in a beauty contest even though she was secretly a Jew in exile
• Amos used to spend his life picking figs and farming sheep until God told him to prophesy to wayward Israel, though untrained to do so
• Elijah was a man of the mountains with no easy charm or sophisticated style when God called him to an exciting mission to his nation at her hour of great crisis
• Rahab was a high class call girl who was a key person in rescuing God's spies from certain death, and became an ancestor of Jesus
• Gideon was an angry young man hiding in a hole in the ground arguing with God about the need for a rescuer when God said, "It's you!"

God will call a person, and wait for them to accept their mission. As we see with Jonah, sometimes He will stop the programme to wait for you to be ready. He has his "sleeper agents" everywhere awaiting the time for their wake-up call.

But be assured, He will call you if He has not done so already. You can make a key difference as a man or woman of God in His world. It may be in church leadership, it may be in schools, hospitals, or the world of technology and science. You could be called to clean up the arts, write new music, confront corruption or provide homes for the poor. Whatever it is, God has an endless portfolio of opportunities to serve. He knows who you are and where you are. He knows what would fit you best; all you need to do is make yourself available to Him and obey the call. The late American preacher Dr. Donald Grey Barnhouse of Tenth Presbyterian Church, Philadelphia, once asserted, "It's impossible for a Christian who wants to know the will of God for his life not to know it."

So we must get ready! There is coming a day when all of God's sleeping agents will be woken up from their unfulfilled lives of merely blending into the background, holding down a dead end job, or aimlessly wandering from place to place, will hear a new call to action. God has created you with the ability to love, think, work and pray. All of heaven and earth is standing on tiptoe for the sons and daughters of God to be revealed, and your time is coming.

"For all creation is waiting eagerly for that future day when God will reveal who his children really are." (Romans 8:19 NLT)

6. Don't Miss Your Destiny

(Jonah 2:8)

If only Jonah had understood that it was impossible to flee from the presence of God! He had heard the call to Nineveh and responded by running in the opposite direction, hiding away on a ship full of foreign sailors bound for a land far away. He had then fallen asleep in the hold, initially oblivious to the storm sent from heaven to wake him up.

God was on the move, and He was shaking Jonah back into his destiny.

Psalm 139 affirms the truth that there is nowhere we can go to separate ourselves from the Spirit of God.

"Where shall I go from Your Spirit?
Or where shall I flee from Your presence?
If I ascend to heaven, You are there!
If I make my bed in Sheol, You are there!
If I take the wings of the morning

and dwell in the uttermost parts of the sea,

even there Your hand shall lead me,

and Your right hand shall hold me." (Psalm 139:7-10)

Jonah had been determined to set a different course for his life from the one God had called him to, not realising that it would leave him unfulfilled, vulnerable and miserable. For life to be fruitful and joyful, Jonah needed to be walking in the Spirit into the destiny God had planned for him. As the storm raged, a new stirring began in the depths of his soul. As he was soon to pray from the belly of the great fish,

"Those who cling to worthless idols turn away from God's love for them." (Jonah 2:8 NIV)

The message that lies at the heart of this narrative is one of warning to those who are in danger of jeopardizing their earthly destiny in becoming distracted by false goals and promises of fake fruitfulness. Turning away from God and replacing Him with something else is a form of idolatry. Jonah was facing the ugly truth about his selfish motivations, disobedience, arrogance and his unfaithfulness to God. He had probably begun to first encounter it in the cries of the sailors who, knowing already how Jonah was running from the Lord as he had told them himself, questioned him thus:

"Tell us on whose account this evil has come upon us. What is your occupation? And where do you come from? What is your country? And of what people are you?" (1:8)

"What is this that you have you done? (1:10)

"What shall we do to you, that the sea may quiet down for us?" (1:11)

Jonah could no longer ignore the truth that by changing the direction of his life, he had not only been unsuccessful in fleeing the presence of God, but he had exposed himself and the sailors to His undeniable wrath.

The purpose of your life

You are not here by chance, but by choice: *God's choice*. He has designed you *with* a purpose and *for* a purpose in order to advance His rule in this sinful and fallen world that He originally designed to be holy and pure. No one else can do what God has planned for you to do and running away from this, as Jonah found out, will not bring peace and rest. Only His plans for you will give you hope not despair, and they will lead you into a good future, not a dead end wilderness of wasted life and final disappointment and regrets.

"For I know the plans I have for you, declares the Lord, plans for welfare and not for evil, to give you a future and a hope." (Jeremiah 29:11)

How easy it is to rationalise an independent autonomy when it comes to the direction of our lives. We convince ourselves that God's will for us is marginal, off-target, negative and restrictive. We believe that He will call us to do something we will hate doing, alongside people we cannot stand to be with.

So we turn our backs on Him, not realising that in doing so we are rejecting the very things we are most seeking. Jonah knew that it was those who clung to the Lord who would experience His love because it is only the Lord who knows what is best for each one of us. He knows you better than you know yourself.

The reality is this: God has already built into each one of us the gifts and talents needed to fulfil His purposes in a particular place, at a particular time in history. He has hard-wired us for this, if we could but see it, and in such a way that this encourages us to become what He has called us to be, often disclosed to us in unforeseen circumstances and specially timed signals. Our choices are meant to line up gladly alongside God's choices because God knows us; He made us and He loves us. Jonah mistakenly believed that God was calling him into a dead end, dangerous and murky place without any consideration for his safety or welfare.

In fact, the opposite was true. God wanted to partner with Jonah to bring about the regeneration of a city and restore such light to it that it would not only be good for Nineveh, it would also prove good for Jonah and perhaps for Israel too. This particular task was something only Jonah could do and it was only when he did what he was told to do, that he would finally feel fully alive.

In the same way, when we ourselves walk with God into our destiny, obeying His call on our lives, we not only bring glory to Him by facilitating change in the environment around us, we will also experience His presence and feel His deep pleasure both in us and in our obedience to Him.

You may have been born out of wedlock or conceived on the back seat of a Ford Escort. But you are not a freak, and God didn't make a mistake in making you. God wanted you. He planned for you. He wasn't taken by surprise with your arrival. You may have been rejected by a parent, or despised by your teachers, probation officer or employer, but God's intentions take precedence over anyone else's plans or schemes for you.

I want to offer some important keys to help you to understand what is in the mind of God that only you can do.

My aim here is to lead you into a personal encounter with the One who knows you better than you know yourself, so imagine these words are written for your eyes only rather than for anyone else you might know.

There are times when we find it easier to believe God's will for someone else rather than taking time to hear His voice for ourselves, so let me encourage you turn your face to Him today and allow Him speak to you. *Don't miss your destiny!*

1. God's plan for you was fashioned before you were created or born

The prophet Jeremiah was born during the last days of Israel's crumbling independence and relentless spiral into ruin. When the Lord originally spoke to him and called him into his prophetic destiny, these were the words He used:

"Before I formed you in the womb I knew you, and before you were born I consecrated you; I appointed you a prophet to the nations." (Jeremiah 1:5)

In other words, God's plan for Jeremiah was not a last minute, hastily executed idea to fill a space in his life at that point. Rather, God had designed Jeremiah's destiny even before he was born.

You have been planned for and thought about in a similar fashion. Before you were a twinkle in the eyes of your parents, God knew you. Your birth was no accident and nor is your destiny a matter of chance. Whatever you have come to believe about your presence in this world, the truth is far more exciting than you can imagine. The God of the universe knows all about you and has a plan for your life. Don't let your own plans intrude to jeopardize or trump God's plans.

It is time to wake up to the truth of God's love for you. It may be that you meant little to your parents and even less to your teachers, causing you to believe the lie that you are worthless and unwanted. God thinks otherwise. He has always known you, and has made you to feel His love, cherishing you as His own. Your past does not define you. Your future is the important factor now, and as you come to Christ, He will heal you and cleanse you from the inside out, making you ready to hear the plans He made especially with you in mind. Recall earlier, that we listed some of the men

and women God called from the back of the line and some out of
the way places. He knows where to find us, and when the time is
right He comes looking.

"He heals the broken-hearted and binds up their wounds."
(Psalm 147:3)

2. Your purpose is determined by God's detailed design of you

Only God has the right to tell you who you are. In a world where
our eyes and ears are perpetually assaulted by someone else's
concept of the perfect body, the best get-rich-quick scheme, or
the perfect lifestyle, we need to return to the truth of who we are
in God's eyes. Jonah thought he knew what would satisfy him in
life. In his defiance, he rejected the call of the One who knew him
better than he knew himself and whose plan would have perfectly
matched Jonah's gifts and personality.

God is the greatest design engineer there is. He delights in
creating unique human beings and calling them to their own
special walk with Him. Your journey with God is unique to you.
Never let anyone define you because that is a role reserved only
for God. The Myers-Briggs personality test can describe you
reasonably accurately, but God knows you best. How easy it is for
the subjective opinions of others to shape us! Parents, siblings,
teachers, friends, co-workers and even wise leaders will all have
a view on who we are based on all manner of things – often as
simple as whether they actually like us or not. Listening to these
opinions can both destroy our confidence and hamper our destiny.
The person you most need to hear from is God.

Let God define you!

I learned long ago that I am hard wired in a particular way.
God has designed me to be fascinated by the big philosophical
questions around the meaning of life and the origins of the human

race. As a young boy, I was compelled by the fascinating world of science fiction and popular sci-fi series like *The Outer Limits* or *Doctor Who*. I would ponder about the stars overhead and what was really "out there". In my youth, I was inextricably drawn to Jesus Christ and when I became a Christian I began to devour the Bible as well as books by such "giants" as C.H. Spurgeon, Francis Schaeffer, John Stott and Dr. Martyn Lloyd-Jones. In 1969, when I was barely 16 years of age, I heard John Stott speak at Keswick. All the threads of my life up to that point drew together, and the call of God rang clearly in my heart as John Stott taught on four consecutive mornings through Paul's letter, 2 Timothy. I knew then that God had made me for a life-calling to Christian ministry as a pastor-teacher and gospel preacher. I had found my life's purpose. This has never left me or seriously wavered since then.

Do you think this is an accident or a freak of nature? No! I came off God's drawing board with all the components latent but intact, only awaiting the right moment for them to be activated so that I could be made ready for a fuller life with my Creator. Some of the wiring may have become a bit knotted or broken over the years due to my own foolish choices or undesirable circumstances beyond my control, but God is faithful to ensure that any needed repairs or appropriate unknotting of entangled emotions will happen when we need it.

God has invested great things into the components needed to fulfil your eternal significance. Your purpose is determined by His design not yours, so it is time to believe the truth of this and let Him reveal it to you. Sin or pain may have temporarily obscured the truth, but when you stop protesting and return to Him with a contrite and expectant heart, you will find out both what He has made you for, and how deeply He loves you and the lives of those connected to you who you will eventually effect for the better.

God does not see you as flawed and cracked; you are made in His image and you are of perfect design. All you need is for Him to restore that design by His powerful grace.

"So God created man in His own image, in the image of God He created him; male and female He created them." (Genesis 1:27)

3. Your planned purpose explains your true but hidden potential

Each one of us has latent abilities and dormant gifts that are waiting to be unblocked and channelled productively. Our potential may be hidden, but God knows it is there and He wants us to be plugged into His purposes right now so the power and potential can be released. It is similar to the process of inserting a battery into an appliance. Until the point where the connection is made, the battery is not fulfilling the potential for which it was made and nor is the appliance.

Do you want to connect to the purposes God has for you life? You may think you have nothing to give and God has discarded you as worthless. This is as far from the truth as you can get. Jesus has bought you with the priceless blood of His own life on the cross because He considers you are worth it. He does not ignore you and has not preferred His design of another person to His design of you. He has plans for both you and them! The potential in you is as full and rich as every other person; it is what you choose to do with this potential that will determine the direction and fruitfulness of your life.

God will lead you step by step into all He has called you to be. Jonah was scared of the consequences of following the call to Nineveh, but God was not going to abandon him and leave him to cope alone. Neither was God asking Jonah to do something for which he was totally ill-equipped, because over the years He had prepared Jonah for such a challenge as Nineveh. With God's guidance, Jonah would be safe on this mission, but Jonah was unconvinced, arrogantly assuming he knew better than God.

It is time to get plugged in to God's vision for your life and begin to unblock your potential. Begin to train for it, study for it, work towards it and serve in some obvious ways that relate to it. Remember that Satan will be focused on throwing all manner of things in your way to distract or alarm you, but stand firm in the truth of who God has made you to be and let Him guide you, leaning on these words from the prophet Isaiah,

"And your ears shall hear a word behind you, saying, 'This is the way, walk in it,' when you turn to the right or when you turn to the left." (Isaiah 30:21)

4. God's purpose is nestled inside your nature and nurture

Your nature is made up of a mix of qualities that belong to you by birth, by parentage and heritage, as well as through God's construction of both events around you, and His supernatural work in you. The unique combination of elements that combine to make you who you are means that you will have preferences, likes and dislikes, along with some things that will come more naturally to you than others.

God wants you to discover what you do well naturally. What is easy for you? What do you love to do? Where do you feel most comfortably in your element? Conversely, what feels alien to you? When do you feel uninspired, incapacitated or restricted?

Jonah was a preacher. He had already spent many years of his life relaying positive messages from God and it was what he did best. To all intents and purposes, being a prophet of God came naturally to him. It fitted like a glove. Yet, with the call to Nineveh, Jonah rejected the will of God and plunged himself into a tumultuous world of confusion where nothing worked and everything was irksome. The landlubber tried to be a sailor, and he ended up all at sea! God had not called Jonah to something beyond his anointing or outside of his nature, but something that matched his personality and abilities. Until he realigned himself to this divine call, he would never be at peace.

Likewise, God will not call you to something you do not already have the capacity to enjoy or draw great fulfilment from. How easily we assume that God will call us to an inhospitable place crawling with deadly snakes and huge spiders, when we have a morbid fear of both! Leave that to David Attenborough! How easily we believe the lie that God will ignore our preferences and unique nature for the sake of His own agenda. We leave ourselves in a place of limbo when we fail to understand that the call of God for our lives is full of promise, and full of grace, and usually aligns us with that which we always wanted to do, if only in our dreams. He knows your nature and He knows what comes naturally to you. When God is in the call, you will excel at everything you do. Not only that, but you will find your passion for it increases, your connection to people becomes stronger, and the favour on your life can be seen by everyone you meet.

Are you currently living your dream with God? Jonah turned away from his dream and it was then that his worst nightmare began. He was no more in his element as a sailor than he was as a deep-sea diver, and his life would not be at rest until he returned to what came naturally or rather, supernaturally to him. In chapter 2 Jonah would come to understand and confess that those who go outside of God's best for their lives forfeit the grace to live it well. God has a perfect plan for every person in His Church and in His world and He will not make any of us do something we have no passion for, unless he changes our passions. He gave us our passions, so why would He ignore them for the sake of

His own agenda for us unless our very make-up soon aligns with that secret agenda? God is not selfish, He is loving and kind and when we walk in His purposes for us, we will begin to understand more of the depths of this truth (Isaiah 48:15; Ephesians 1:15-21; Philippians 1:6-11).

So find out what God wants you to do. I guarantee you will eventually grow to love it, regardless of any initial reluctance!

5. God's destiny for you matches your gifts and abilities

As a prophet of God, Jonah could both hear from heaven and communicate clearly and powerfully to His people. God had given Jonah the ability to speak to the hardest hearts and touch them with the truth. When he fled to Joppa and set sail to Tarshish, he went outside of his proper sphere of influence and gifting and began to lose his prophet's identity. Jonah was never supposed to be sailing away to a foreign land because God had already gifted him to be His messenger in a different place for a different purpose.

Creation is full of creatures specifically designed and gifted by God for a particular task. Owls, for instance, have large and sensitive eyes fashioned for optimum effectiveness in their nocturnal hunt. Woodpeckers have a precision muscle system in their necks designed for hammering and drilling into the bark of a tree at a rate of over two hundred times a minute without brain damage. Our Creator God has made a world full of fascinating and beautiful mechanisms that balance and dovetail together to give Him pleasure. Not only that, but when He created these manifold wonders and saw that it was all so good, He placed humanity there to enjoy it along with Him.

In 1981, the multi award winning film *Chariots of Fire* was released to worldwide and Oscar-winning acclaim, telling the story of the Scottish athlete and missionary Eric Liddell who won gold for Great Britain in the 400 meters sprint at the 1924 Paris Olympic Games. The race he won was not one he had trained for. As the heats for the 100 meters were scheduled on a Sunday, the one day of the week he would not race as he observed it as a day of rest, the Lord's day, he found himself unable to enter the race he had prepared for. He had to compete in an alternative race the day after. By all accounts, he should not have won the race, let alone set a new world record of 47.6 seconds. But he knew God was with him and when his sister Jenny challenged him on his delay to follow the call of God to China in favour of the Olympics, he answered her, "Jenny, God made me fast, and when I run I feel His pleasure." God had made Eric Liddell an extraordinary athlete, but he was also to become an exemplary missionary to China in God's good time. In both aspects, God was glorified by his life.

You can be a great witness for Christ simply by doing what you are good at doing to God's glory. You may be a great mathematician, a proficient linguist, highly creative with words or music, a wonderful mother, a caring doctor. You may be doing exactly what you are gifted to do, and in doing it you feel the pleasure of God along with the anointing of His Holy Spirit. Don't stop doing it because you feel the pressure to go somewhere else, or human goading to change track. Let neither internal struggles nor the opinions of others allow you to become temporarily unsettled. It is primarily God's smile you are looking for.

6. Where God guides, He provides

There are many people who strive to do uncommanded work that God never intended them to do. Such people genuinely want to obey the call of God but have somehow become confused and unclear as to what their specific call is. This can happen for many different reasons. More often than not it is rooted in a fear of lack or worry about insufficient financial or other resources.

When we allow our human reasoning to replace the creative voice God, our expectation of supernatural intervention for provision becomes smaller and smaller. Jonah never really prospered outside of the will of God, and neither will we.

The Bible says,

"A man's gift makes room for him and brings him before the great." (Proverbs 18:16)

Which means that God gives grace to open formerly closed doors in front of us when we live in the freedom of who He has made us to be, and what He is capable of arranging, when needed. He is not confined to the systems of this world or subject to the financial institutions that control it. He will provide for us when we let Him lead us. Where God leads, He feeds. Where God guides, He provides. If we do His will, He will foot the bill!

The nineteenth century missionary James Hudson Taylor once voiced his conviction, "God's work done in God's way will never lack God's provision to maintain it." In other words, God will give you the money, people, energy, ideas, enthusiasm and creativity to do whatever He asks you to do. You will discover that people listen to you, follow you and want to serve alongside you. In His generosity and love, God will not allow His call on your life to become an albatross around your neck, sapping the energy and life out of you and making you wish you were doing something else.

God's resources will chase you; you will not have to chase them. If you have not yet gathered the right people around you or sufficient funding to fulfil His call, be assured that He will send the people and necessary finance to you. The tasks into which He calls you should never be fruitless or make you fretful. Rather, they should give you joy and peace, as well as passion in your soul and fire in your belly.

God has prepared both us and our gifts for a place of His choosing, and we will always feel a sense of displacement and unease until we finally get there. Are you ready to truly be and become the person who God made you to be? Will you, with Jonah, acknowledge the extraordinary grace that can only be found when you are in the centre of His will for your life?

"Those who pay regard to vain idols forsake their hope of steadfast love. But I with the voice of thanksgiving will sacrifice to You; what I have vowed I will pay. Salvation belongs to the Lord!" (Jonah 2:8-9)

7. Jonah in the Deep

(Jonah 1:7-2:10)

"Love that gives upward is worship, love that goes outward is
affection, love that stoops is grace."
–Donald Grey Barnhouse (1895-1960)

After hearing the call of God to go to Nineveh and subsequently
avoiding it, Jonah forfeited all three of these dimensions of love.
He abandoned the upward worship of God, withheld outward
affection from the people of Nineveh and relinquished his
responsibility to show God's grace to an errant imperilled city
under the threat of destruction.

Jonah had seemingly missed his destiny through his own
selfishness, fear and rebellion. God had executed a plan, which
uniquely fitted his character and could potentially bring tremendous
favour on a city in jeopardy. All that was needed was Jonah's co-
operation. But as we know from the account, the prophet had
decided to run as far away from God as he possibly could.

In chapter six, we considered the advantages of recognising and implementing the plans and purposes of God in our lives. We saw how God plants a sense of destiny in all of us, whoever we are, and whatever our natural gifting. Tragic then that so many dismiss these intimations, or deliberately ignore them as wishful thinking. We saw, too, the lengths to which God was prepared to go to call Jonah back to his destiny via the call of the wild and the call of the world as he faced the biggest storm of his life.

There are times when God gently calls a person back onto the right path, especially if they have wandered aimlessly away over time. However, if the rebellion has been wilful and strong, as in Jonah's case, God will characteristically lead that person to a crisis point, which will more often than not involve a death of some kind. God will often challenge us to die to our own plans, to our own wilfulness, and to our own autonomy and childish independence. Ultimately, we are required to die to sin – to acknowledge that we have allowed the enemy to lead us away from the truth of who we are in Christ, and therefore into conflict with His best intentions for us.

This is exactly what was about to happen to Jonah.

In the New Testament there are many important passages in the epistles of both Peter and Paul that explain how, before we converted to Christ, the sin of rebellion was uppermost in our lives, and how an independent spirit can, if allowed, continue to harass us and lead us astray.

I want to give three key examples.

1. Ephesians 2:1-5

"And you were dead in the trespasses and sins in which you once walked, following the course of this world, following the prince of the power of the air, the spirit that is now at work in the sons of disobedience – among whom we all once lived in the passions of our flesh, carrying out the desires of the body and the mind, and were by nature children of wrath, like the rest of mankind. But God, being rich in mercy, because of the great love with which He loved us, even when we were dead in our trespasses, made us alive together with Christ – by grace you have been saved."

With characteristic probity, Paul tells the church in Ephesus that prior to salvation in Christ their lives were utterly dead to all that mattered. Our most deadly enemies are *the world* (human society as it runs itself without any reference to God), *the flesh* (corrupt human nature at enmity with God), and *the devil* (Satanic powers fuelled by hatred of all that comes from God). Unbelievers are usually oblivious to this conflict. The prevailing atmosphere of godlessness in their world has kept them from enjoying the fullness of life that God had destined for them. Like dead fish, all man can do is float downstream without God.

The same is true for us today. In a world where the name of God is used more readily as a blasphemous expletive than in awed songs of worship, Satan has free reign to behave like a puppet master, pulling the strings of lives that move only in accordance with his promptings and direction. Only the resurrection power of Christ can break these mighty forces and usher us into a new world of spiritual freedom and access to God. This is quite literally a resurrection from death to life.

2. Colossians 2:13

"And you, who were dead in your trespasses and the uncircumcision of your flesh, God made alive together with Him, having forgiven us all our trespasses..."

Paul writes to the Colossian church in a similar vein to the passage from Ephesians as he alludes to the corpse-like nature of life prior to salvation. Spiritual death is akin to physical death, in which the body has no vital signs and is totally unresponsive to stimuli. Our own treacherous nature, suppressed guilt that refuses any real accountability to God and the condemning power of God's broken Law have all prevented us from saving ourselves, or in many cases even recognising the need for rescue at all. It is God alone who has made us alive again by Christ's crucifixion and resurrection, which has permanently bound and set limits to the force of the powers of darkness and continues to set the prisoners free. In Him, we are resurrected into new life, so that once doomed prisoners of war become liberated to serve God once again.

3. 1 Peter 1:18-19

"...Knowing that you were ransomed from the futile ways inherited from your forefathers, not with perishable things such as silver or gold, but with the precious blood of Christ, like that of a lamb without blemish or spot."

Here, Peter is explaining how our former lifestyles without Christ were utterly selfish, temporal and futile. They were as far from any true or lasting worth as it was possible to be. Before we were saved, we were on the refuse dump, trashed and discarded as obsolete having failed to live for the purposes and functions we were created for, so that all that was awaiting us was the eternal incinerator of hell itself. But thank God, He is in the salvage business! In this case it is people not things that can be recycled. Only the blood of Jesus could have paid the ransom sufficient to rescue us from such a dreadful state and terrible end.

Scripture tells us how, in order to be released from the lostness of a life in sin and rebellion against God, something deep, lasting and radical has to happen to us for this fate to be undone. It is nothing less than the substitutionary death of Jesus Christ and our death to self that will release us from the dungeon of our own making, into a life of spiritual resurrection and restored destiny. But first, we have to encounter the reality of how our lives are affected by being at odds with the will of God. Like Jonah, God will face us with the truth of the danger we are in as we run away so recklessly from His call. It is only in this frightening place that we fully encounter the misery rebellion brings and awaken to the futility of life without God.

For Jonah, such dreadful events unfolded before him in two distinct stages. The first was *danger* and the second *death*.

Danger (Jonah 1:10-16)

There are basically three types of people in the world:

• Those who characteristically take action and make things happen
• Those who stand by "rubber-necking" and watch things happen
• Those who seem oblivious and wonder what on earth is happening!

Jonah belonged to category three, asleep in the hold. He had moved from being a prophet in Israel, one who could hear what God was saying and then make things happen, to a slumbering cruise passenger oblivious to all that was happening around him. With the decision to flee from and lose touch with God, he had lost himself. His purpose in life was messed up and confused as he sailed furtively to Tarshish, but without any real direction any longer in his life. Suddenly, events took a catastrophic turn for the worse, for the simple reason that he had put his own plans before the plans of God. As the sea became rougher and rougher, the danger escalated not just for Jonah but also for all those on board. This was no mild Mediterranean squall; it was a storm unlike any the sailors had ever witnessed before. It was a weather system they could do nothing about other than to throw the cargo overboard to help stabilise the ship. Our disobedience as God's people often has the knock-on effect of messing up other people's lives and plans too.

How often has this been the case in our own lives? Over my life so far in church ministry, I have known some passionate zealots for God, intense about the power of the gospel and deeply committed to leading unbelievers to Christ. Whilst the focus was noble, their passions would sometimes mask unresolved, deeper issues of the heart such as an independent or graceless attitude, pride or arrogance. When these un-Christlike character traits were left unattended and unchanged, I saw first hand how a life can spiral into despair and wreckage as storms rushed in.

God wants us wholly, and He also wants us whole! It is only when we submit everything to Christ that we truly find ourselves. In our arrogance and determination we so easily lose the plot and also lose ourselves, as Jonah soon found out. When lots were cast and they fell on Jonah, it was the beginning of God's revelation about who and what he had allowed himself to become. One such man I knew, was a little short-statured zealot who hung around pubs to tell customers of their need for a Saviour. But his independence, ambiguous attitudes, resistance to advice, pride in "always knowing what's best" and a refusal to receive input and correction, all placed him in serious danger. His love-hate relationship with other Christians and even the Church, rendered him vulnerable and Satan took advantage of this. His drift away from God became relentless, finally wrecking his marriage, damaging the faith of his children, and ending with him becoming a full-time barman at one of the clubs he used to try to rescue drunks from. His once vibrant testimony was silent for many years. This highlights the dangers of running from God, the God who is not at war with us, but rather with the sin that lands us in a state of conflict with Him. Very often, even unbelievers are shocked by the fallen state of backslidden believers, and this would soon be the case with Jonah's crew of terrified sailors.

"And they said to one another, 'Come, let us cast lots, that we may know on whose account this evil has come upon us.' So they cast lots, and the lot fell on Jonah." (Jonah 1:7)

God had found him out. This was no chance lottery, since the hand of God had manipulated events to expose Jonah's sin to everyone present. Jonah's number came up. The dice were already loaded against him! Proverbs 16:33 says,

"The lot is cast into the lap, but its every decision is from the Lord."

This is an Old Testament acknowledgement of the importance of God's hand intervening providentially in the lives of those who are seeking direction, whether they are believers or not. Jonah wasn't found out by chance, but by choice – God's choice. God was not so much after Jonah himself but his folly and sin. It is one of God's greatest mercies when he finally finds us out.

Sin is our worst enemy. It is sin that keeps us silent when we are required to speak; it is sin that paralyzes us with fear, and sin that makes us do foolish and idiotic things. We deceive ourselves if we think we can tolerate sin in our lives with impunity. God hates sin and wants us to be free of it. God doesn't hate *you*, just *your sin*. He will not stop looking for you, pursuing you with the intent to restore you along with the truth of who you are in His eyes, then reclaiming the destiny He has planned for you. No matter how determined you are to stay lost, God knows where to find you and will make Himself known to you in whatever ways He chooses.

This was not pleasant for Jonah, and it will not be pleasant for us sometimes. In turning up the heat and exposing the danger we have become to others, and ourselves, God shines a light on our character and paves the way for restoration, often with tears. It's very painful for us when God turns up the heat. But the alternative is freezing to death in cold, silent waters.

Jonah was suffering from a form of amnesia and needed a shock to awaken him and help recover his memory. How easily we allow our individual and collective amnesia to seep into our consciousness so that we believe all manner of lies about who we really are. Thank God for His Word! When Scripture tells us,

"For the Lord disciplines the one He loves, and chastises every son whom He receives." (Hebrews 12:6)

We need to believe it! Occasionally I like to translate it as, "Whom the Lord loves, He beats the hell out of!", and I don't think this is going too far.

As the angry sailors begin their aggressive interrogation of Jonah like special interrogators with a rubber truncheon, questioning him unrelentingly about his identity, his orignins, and his occupation, it is as if God Himself is pounding him with the same questions. It is as if the prophet of God is on trial in both an earthly and heavenly courtroom. A bewildered Jonah is being forced to not only admit the truth to the sailors, but also to himself and to God as he answers them,

"I am a Hebrew, and I fear the Lord, the God of heaven, who made the sea and the dry land." (Jonah 1:9 ESV)

As the sea grew rougher and rougher, God faced Jonah with the turmoil of the position in which he had found himself, forcing him to wake up and come back to his senses. There were things in Jonah that needed to die. Spiritually, he was all at sea, but God was making a way in both the sea and in the storm.

Have you been in any trouble or danger recently? Are you confused by the events of your life? Is everything going wrong for you? Perhaps everything you put your hand to seems to disintegrate or dissolve into nothing? Have you taken the time to ask God whether there is anything about your life that is heading in the wrong direction and will never turn out right? Could it be time for you to turn around and reverse direction?

God will not hesitate to expose us to painful things in order to get our attention. He does this because He loves us, which may appear inconsistent with our fear and pain at the time, until we remember that it is the sin in us that He can't tolerate, not our own selves. The invitation to repent will come at key moments of our life in order to allow us to turn around to face a better way - God's way. The only way that fits how we were designed and indeed, the grain of the universe itself.

If this is you today, I want to invite you to pray this prayer right now as we continue on through the chapter.

"Lord, I believe you are exposing me to my own sin and wilfulness at this time in my life. I can feel the danger of the storms all around me and I acknowledge my part in them. I understand that my choices to go my own way and do my own thing have sometimes taken me far from You, and from Your plans for me. I also know that You have never stopped looking for me because You love me and know what is best for me. I repent of my self-centred approach to life; of the lie that I can live it independently of You, by pursuing goals and dreams that do not have You at their heart. You are my God and I would like You to please forgive me and restore me. Amen."

Death (Jonah 2:1-10)

"He said to them, 'Pick me up and hurl me into the sea; then the sea will quiet down for you, for I know it is because of me that this great tempest has come upon you.'" (Jonah 1:12)

In the midst of the raging storm, Jonah did not bother beseeching God to calm the wind and waves. He did not intercede for a miracle, or even tell the sailors to sit tight as it would all soon be over. He knew that just as he was the cause of the storm, he would be the one who ended it. Jonah knew that God wanted nothing less than his death. By being hurled into the sea to almost certain death, Jonah would assuage the wrath of God and the sailors would be saved. In some profound way, this awesome reality qualified Jonah to become a type or forerunner of Christ himself. Dying our death, Christ saved our lives.

Prior to Jonah's request, the sailors had done everything humanly possible to prevent a mass drowning. The narrative tells of a frantic attempt to row back to shore (1:13), which was prevented due to ever worsening conditions. Cargo was jettisoned (1:5), and despite each man's appeal to his own god for mercy, there was no change. Human effort, sacrificial hard work, and even religious practices like prayer do not buy salvation for anyone. Salvation is God's prerogative, a work of unmerited grace toward ruined lives that would be doomed apart from His initiative and intervention.

The sailors did their best, but the wrath of God was not that easily assuaged. The same is true today. No political party, politician, educator, economist or religious guru can "row us back to land" and put an end to the storms that rage across the nations of the world. The futility of our attempts to placate God take precedence over the simple truth that we, His fallen creatures, have not afforded Him the honour and authority that is due to Him. All of our noble schemes and elaborate ideas to improve society, from promises to cancel Third World debt to praying in the streets after a suicide bomb attack, will never change the fact that on the whole, God is regularly and systematically ignored. It is akin to putting a sticking plaster on a malignant tumour that festers and grows under that flimsy covering. The problems we encounter are like a cancer in our society and the only remedy is the direct intervention of a supernatural loving God. Good intentions and human counter-measures will simply not suffice.

In Jeremiah 6:14 God complains through His prophet saying,

"They have healed the wound of My people lightly saying, 'Peace, peace,' when there is no peace."

In other words, real peace comes at a great price. It is not cheap. For some reason, the Church is often at the forefront of thinking that God is some benign, bearded old grandfather in the sky who can't remember where He put His pipe and slippers. We are sold the image of a bumbling, mumbling old man who loves everyone and wouldn't harm a fly.

Try telling that to Jonah!

God was going to turn things around, but He was going to do it His way. Jonah was not going to be given a well-deserved sabbatical in sun-soaked Tarshish because God had called Him to do something important and there would be no peace for Jonah until he fully submitted to His will. In addition, there would be no peace for Nineveh until they repented of their wickedness. But that outcome not only depended upon God's actions, but also Jonah's.

The price of peace

Peace is just a buzzword unless it is centred on the cross and on the bloody death of Christ and the radical change it makes in the life of the individual.

The moment that Jonah is thrown overboard, peace returns. God's wrath is calmed in the very moment when Jonah is offered to the waves as a substitute for the crew. The message given to the sailors by Jonah is thus an advance echo of the work of the cross: the man of God must die so that others can live. Surely Jonah is one of the most charismatically gifted evangelists in the whole of the Old Testament!

So too, just as Jonah cries,

"For You cast me into the deep,
into the heart of the seas,
and the flood surrounded me;
all Your waves and your billows
passed over me." (Jonah 2:3)

We know it was not Pontius Pilate who put Jesus to death, nor was it the screams of the Sanhedrin that killed him, but it was "The will of the Lord to crush Him;" (Isaiah 53:10)

It was God's sentence of death upon the lives of Jonah, and more importantly, Jesus himself, that confounds the popular opinion that God is a benevolent has-been, incapable of anger, passive and remote. How easily we distance ourselves from the ministries of men like Jonah and Jeremiah who illustrate the divine strategy to,

"Pluck up and to break down, to destroy and to overthrow, to build and to plant." (Jeremiah 1:10)

There are times when we need to come to the realisation that the Father's sentence of death is upon us and all of our feeble attempts to save ourselves and others. Jesus said, "Truly, truly, I say to you, unless a grain of wheat falls into the earth and dies, it remains alone; but if it dies, it bears much fruit." (John 12:24)

We are more comfortable with God as a builder and not a destroyer, but the Bible is very clear that in order to gain life, there must be death. God will then remove the corpse, which is old and effete, replacing it with His own living, breathing body, the Church, now raised and pulsing with life this side of Christ's resurrection. Flowing from the negatives of judgement and death comes the freshness and positive outcomes of new life and peace.

Cosmetic surgery?

In both Church and State we have turned against God. We have employed the same techniques that we watch on reality make-over shows on television, designed to improve people's appearance or restore derelict institutions so that they become more attractive and palatable. Similarly, as Christians, we often look at our flabby churches and think that a few cosmetic changes such as changing the layout of the meeting hall, introducing new songs, or dressing down in T-shirt and jeans will somehow make us more contemporary and attract people in. We pay lip service to the Holy Spirit while in reality, very little has actually changed deep down in our hearts. We run on empty traditions and take part in dreary, powerless, un-anointed services. We pride ourselves on looking good from the outside when we are often decaying inside.

But God looks at the heart!

He has watched His Church in our nation decline in numbers and in power. He has grieved over our rebellion and compromise and been angered by our fake, play-acting hypocrisy.

Like Jonah, the Church is now beyond human help and it is God Himself who has sentenced us to die, in order that we might live. There is no easy passage from failure to success or from withering decline to sudden flourishing, because we have not cheerfully volunteered to experience and then pass on the undesirable divine remedy.

God is calling us to die to self. We need to lay down our own prestige, reputation, self-reliance and self-will, then repent of the error of our ways in thinking that we can run church as we want to, preaching messages we decided to preach, that never disturb the status quo or offend anyone, whilst Jesus is often excluded and standing outside our lukewarm church programmes, persistently knocking at the door of His own church until someone consents to welcome His entry. He is saying in effect, "Can I have my church back please?" (Revelation 3:20). *Our hope lies in God and God alone to save us from death!*

Baptism

In effect, Jonah went through a dramatic water baptism by immersion of his body and soul in the swirling waters of the Mediterranean Sea. In the ancient world the Greek word *baptizo* described an overwhelming experience of being completely soaked with water, a total swamping or immersion. It was also a word used of a man drowned at sea or the sinking of a ship that had keeled over in a storm and lunged to the sea bed.

This same word was also alluded to by Jesus metaphorically in Mark's gospel when He refers to His coming plunge into the overwhelming flood of suffering on the cross (Mark 10:38). The concept was also written about by the Psalmist in these verses, which were echoed and alluded to by Jonah in chapter 2:1-9,

"Save me, O God!
For the waters have come up to my neck.
I sink in deep mire,
where there is no foothold;
I have come into deep waters,
and the flood sweeps over me." (Psalm 69:1-2)

"Deliver me
from sinking in the mire;
let me be delivered from my enemies
and from the deep waters.
Let not the flood sweep over me,
or the deep swallow me up,
or the pit close its mouth over me." (Psalm 69:14-15)

Have you been both physically and spiritually baptized and sunk into Jesus yet, and has the Trinity been named over you in that plunge He commanded for all His followers (Mark 16:15-16)? I would like to recommend this to you! When you are baptized in Jesus' name, your old life is officially buried and your new life is officially commenced by rising in newness out of the depths, to begin the exciting journey into your earthly and heavenly destiny with God. Baptism is both a bath for the dirty and a burial for the dead. It makes way for a completely new beginning, drawing a line under a wayward past.

With Jonah, let your cry be heard also, as you seal your commitment to Christ with renewed vows of obedience to Him:

"But I with the voice of thanksgiving
will sacrifice to You;
what I have vowed I will pay.
Salvation belongs to the Lord!" (Jonah 2:9)

8. Jonah Lost at Sea

(Jonah 1:13-2:7)

The book of Jonah was written to challenge little people with shrunken minds and deep prejudices, who have grown inward looking, self-centred, accustomed to a parochial outlook on life and often walled-up within their own limited concerns in some kind of "fortress mentality", oblivious to the plight of others. It is impossible to read Jonah carefully and simultaneously hold on to the view that life is dull, predictable or bland, whilst still retaining a small vision that anticipates few surprises from God. Here is a story bursting with "bigness". Contained within it's four short chapters the Hebrew word for "big" is used fourteen times, describing a big city, a big storm, the big fear that gripped the sailors, a big fish sent to swallow Jonah, the prophet's big anger and eventually a big revival in the city of Nineveh, and so on. As we read it, we are challenged to step outside the boundaries of what is counted as normal and enter a world where anything is possible. God wants to break our small minded thinking, our low expectations and our blinkered view of ourselves so that with Jonah, we turn around to face Him, gasping for air and reeling from the shock of new possibilities.

When Jonah booked his ticket to Tarshish, he had no idea that God had planned to arrest him. He had every reason to expect a safe passage on a benign sea, casually befriending foreign sailors who knew nothing of his past and nothing of his God, on his way to a new life across the Mediterranean sea. Jonah may have been out of the reach of an internet provider, but he was never out of God's reach. God's eyes were on him, and he was to encounter the wrath of heaven at the very point he thought he had slipped away unnoticed and forgotten, now safely under the radar.

We are never lost to God. We may try to keep a low profile and stay small, ignoring His call and running relentlessly from our destiny, but God will never stop pursuing us or challenging our fears and rebellion to the point where we cry out and acknowledge His perfect will for our lives.

Black comedy

The message of Jonah is made all the more poignant and powerful by the use of dark humour, the kind of humour that makes us laugh even at ourselves. To illuminate our thinking, God will often hold a mirror up in front of us to highlight the ridiculous nature of our attempts to remain content living within a narrow world we want to control. The futility of Jonah's efforts to run away, and the peculiarities of his behaviour at key points on the journey, are laughable to us, and yet as we read them we have a nagging realization that all of us have either already or could possibly in the future, act in exactly the same way. The text is amusing to us but it is designed to awaken and convict us.

We have seen the big joke of Jonah's attempt to get away from God by boarding a ship destined for land far away. But don't we do the same? I have known people who have tried to join the foreign legion or travel to Timbuktu in an attempt to flee from the call of God impinging upon a particularly sensitive area of their lives. Yes, there is some decidedly black humour here, bordering on the absurd comedy of *Monty Python* or *Black Adder*.

Then there is the account of the pagan Phoenician sailors, all with their own gods and rituals of worship, but who, in the thick of a storm come scuttling back to another God for protection. How true of our own lives! We may stray into new alignments to the pet, token gods of the world, occupying our thinking with get-rich-quick schemes, or the pursuit of material things, but when the storm comes we leave everything behind to finally seek God's face again.

The Jonah account is peppered with amusing images of a shivering ship (a "nervous wreck"), an enormous fish, some sack-clothed cattle, a fabulously tall shady plant, a worm with "attitude" and a sulking, belligerent prophet who is given the main part in this comedy of errors. The narrative draws us into its sense of the absurdity of life as any well-mounted farcical theatre performance would do, so that we are forced to ask, "What will happen to Nineveh in the end? Will Jonah live to tell the tale? What will God do?" and most importantly, "What would I do?"

In Joppa, Jonah had taken control of his own destiny by purchasing a ticket to Tarshish. He had tasted a lame, confused and short-lived kind of freedom, but it was only in death and resurrection that he would encounter full freedom, as we are about to find out.

Into the deep

There has been much discussion about what actually happened to Jonah after the sailors jettisoned him overboard. Some would say he supernaturally morphed into an amphibious being, others would say the great fish arrived quickly, swallowing him into a dank pocket of breathable air in its stomach. But I have become convinced that Jonah actually died, not only metaphorically but also literally. As he "went down" originally to Joppa, then to the ship's hold and finally to the depths of the sea, he also went down into Sheol the place of the dead. I believe that, like Christ, Jonah tasted death and burial, only to rise again when the fish vomited him out.

Parallels with Christ

• Jonah's death is not the only parallel to the life of Jesus. There is evidence that he grew up, like Jesus, in a small town near Nazareth and we read in the passage in 2 Kings 14:25 how from quite early on, he also was a star preacher not only in northern Israel but wider afield. In effect, it was a case of "local boy makes good"!

• Although, of course, Jesus never went on the run from the call of His Father, Jonah died a death similar in nature to the Son of God. When he was thrown overboard, he was sacrificed to save the lives of sinners around him who, in the end, were forced to become his killers. In their own words, the sailors had sacrificed an innocent man to avert the wrath of God from falling on them, so they literally sacrificed and killed him in order to save themselves, discerning that this was God's deeper plan.

"Therefore they called out to the Lord, 'O Lord, let us not perish for this man's life, and lay not on us innocent blood, for you, O Lord, have done as it pleased you.'" (Jonah 1:14)

This is exactly what Pontius Pilate and the Sanhedrin would later do with Jesus Christ. These are the words of Caiaphas, High Priest at the time:

"'Nor do you understand that it is better for you that one man should die for the people, not that the whole nation should perish.' He did not say this of his own accord, but being High Priest that year he prophesied that Jesus would die for the nation, and not for the nation only, but also to gather into one the children of God who are scattered abroad." (John 11:50-52)

- Although the nature of Jonah's death was different from that of Christ, in that Jonah was not scourged, beaten and pierced, the prophet was also buried out of sight in a watery, weedy grave only to miraculously rise again three days later. Jesus Himself refers to Jonah in the gospel of Matthew thus:

"For just as Jonah was three days and three nights in the belly of the great fish, so will the Son of Man be three days and three nights in the heart of the earth." (Matthew 12:40)

- By Jonah's death, the ship's crew were literally saved, coming to a knowledge and fear of Yahweh as a result (Jonah 1:16), which has an obvious parallel to the Atonement. The spiritual contagion of a man or woman called by God, as Jonah was, is remarkable. Even when the messenger is in disobedience and rebellion, lost and gone, he or she still has the power to affect people because God will use every situation to open the way for an encounter with His presence. Paradoxically, life is often the surprising outcome of death. The lasting result of both Jonah's and Jesus' deaths was that life could begin again for everyone connected with them.

Dead means dead!

Jonah's departure into the deep and the confines of the sea monster's belly was not a temporary swoon or a limp, near-death experience. We need to understand that he actually died. He sank to the bottom of the Mediterranean Sea, kept in the grip of those dark waters, wrapped in seaweed, motionless and cold. Human beings have the capacity to hold their breath underwater for only a few short minutes before their lungs cry out for oxygen. Drowning occurs very quickly with submerged human beings. Even the world-famous illusionist and stunt performer David Blaine, attempting to hold his breath for a record seven minutes, could only manage a disappointing four minutes in a recent public performance in a glass tank of water.

The footnote to chapter 2 verse 5 in my particular Bible translation describes how the waters entered Jonah's throat. In other words, he gulped down and inhaled pints of water and out came pints of breathable air. Once that exchange had taken place, Jonah was finished. His life "ebbed away" (v7).

Furthermore, Jonah could now see that his destination was in fact the grave, using the Hebrew word *sheol* in chapter 2 verse 2. This word denotes "the abode of the dead", "the grave", the Hebrew equivalent of the Greek concept of Hades – the shadowy underworld whence the dead depart. When Jonah prays as recorded in chapter 2 verses 1-9, he is praying as a disembodied spirit, a dead soul. He is finished, his body is drowned and he is lifeless at the bottom of the sea.

If this is so, then when God sent the big fish, it was not to save him from death, but to protect his body from corruption and from further harm and decay after he had died. The huge fish did not pick Jonah up from the surface to save his life, but from entangled weeds on the sea-bed, where he had already perished.

In preserving Jonah's body, God was protecting him from becoming food for fishes in the same way that the body of Christ was preserved from fly-blown maggots and worms by being laid in the tomb of a rich man. What was needed now was nothing short of a resurrection.

But then, God is the God of resurrection. Only with Him can the dead live again.

No matter how far you have sunk or how dead you feel, God will preserve you and can pick you up again. This is what He had in mind for Jonah all along, so allow the truth of it to sink into your spirit as you reflect on the events to come.

Hard to swallow?

The account of the great fish in the Jonah narrative has become the stuff of legend. For centuries it has fired the imaginations of illustrators and film makers, authors and craftsmen, all beguiled by the story of this monster that could swallow a man whole. Echoes of this story occur in Disney's animation *Pinocchio*, Spielberg's blockbuster *Jaws*, and Israeli artist Eugene Abeshaus' depiction of Jonah disembarking from the fish and landing at Haifa in a *shtetl* coat with two suitcases, looking tired and sick like an immigrant seeking asylum.

In reality, the focus on the fish has trivialized the sober reality of what occurred. As G. Campbell-Morgan once expressed this, "Men have been looking so hard at the great fish they have failed to look at the great God."

Is this too hard for us to believe? Do you struggle to grasp the authentic tale of Jonah's death? Some have certainly doubted the veracity of the story of James Bartlett, but there is no question that creation has within it such animals that consume human beings whole. The anaconda and the crocodile are powerful predators, proven to be capable of swallowing human prey. It may be easier to believe, too, that Jonah simply fainted and was held unconscious in the belly of the fish, but the clear message of death and resurrection in the account itself is impossible to ignore. Whether you concur with my view that Jonah actually died, or not, my challenge to you is to embrace the truth of the wonderful audacity of what God did to restore His servant to the plans He had for him at all costs.

It is not only the visitation of the gulping fish that stretches our imagination; God has arranged a total of eight astonishing miracles in this book. Alluding to them, Alec Motyer comments, "This puts the emphasis where it belongs; there is a sovereign God who controls all things, all powers and means are at His disposal, but His awesome irresistible power is His love at work with even His destructive capacity directed to constructive ends. All of these affirm God's freedom to act in His own world in His own ways." (*The Story of the Old Testament,* p112)

Our hope does not lie in human legends or dumbed down versions of biblical initiatives. Our God is the *living God* who holds creation and its workings in His sovereign hands, moulding it in such a way as to see His will done. Faith is to be based on fact. Difficult as it is for some to believe, the story of Jonah is factual.

The meaning in the storm

It was the tumult that took Jonah into the deep. In that place, he lost all touch with reality, peace and stability and it was unknown to all but God at that point as to whether he would be lost or found.

The same is true for us all. As we encounter life's storms, battered by their ferocity, helplessly caught in their force, rigid with fear at the potential outcome, we can lose our grip on reality and feel like we can't go on. It looks like all is lost. There are no spectators in a storm and it can be an exhausting time for all, as it was for each man on the ship to Tarshish as they fought for their lives. They all had die to false hopes of survival without God.

Unless we allow God to rule and reign in the storms that hit our lives from time to time, we are in serious danger of losing our souls. When Jonah and the sailors acknowledged the sovereignty of God and submitted to His ways, the violent waves ceased, the wind calmed and everything went back to how it was. Or did it? The sober truth is that nothing could ever be the same again for anybody.

The key areas of change were in the sailors, and more importantly, in Jonah. He had died to himself, to his stubborn desire to run his ministry and life his way, and given it all back to God. As a further stunning result, a whole city would live. As with Christ, who died, was buried and rose again to save a whole world, Jonah would proclaim life to a dead and doomed immoral Middle Eastern city.

Only people who have died to self and lived again can proclaim life to others!

Sacrificing self

In nineteenth century Bristol, a Brethren Christian philanthropist by the name of George Müller caught God's heart of compassion for the poor and fatherless children living in his city. Before long he was caring for hundreds of them, trusting God for the resources to meet their needs. Every day he would pray in faith for God to provide, and every day God did just that.

The work was to expand in Britain and overseas so that eventually tens of thousands of children received the care they had been lacking. When he was once asked what was the secret of his great faith and outstanding success, George Müeller answered,

"There was a day when I died, utterly died, died to George Müeller, his opinions, preferences, tastes and will, died to the world, its approval or censure, died to the approval or blame even of my brethren and friends, and since then I have studied only to show myself approved unto God."

This day must come to us all, sooner or later.

Jonah died. He sank under the sea to the point where his eardrums thundered in pain and his lungs emptied of air, and his limbs ceased to flail, the watery grave taking him to a place of solitude and cold darkness. In his aloneness, as the breath ebbed away he came face to face with himself and the realization of what he had done.

When the Father's "sentence of death" comes on the lives of His children to deal with things that are earmarked for final closure, we get time not only to experience the process by which God does this, we also get time to assess the effects of it on our lives, and to come to terms with the Father's severe dealings with us. It is a sober but ultimately enriching experience, and one we can never forget.

My own death

Some years ago, I had my own encounter with the belly of the fish when I descended into the greatest trial of my life.

I had just returned from a taxing three-week speaking trip to India and was looking forward to preaching at the two Easter meetings that first Sunday back at my home church, one of which was a baptismal service. At 7.45am on that morning, I had already showered, dressed and was getting myself prepared to preach when I felt some unusual twinges of pain in my middle abdomen, just under the rib cage. Within thirty minutes I was rolling in the worst agony I had ever experienced, gripped by a debilitating unbearable pain. My wife Ruth called the ambulance and I went for emergency examination and treatment, only to be admitted to Intensive Care in the local hospital where I fought for my life for the next five months.

I was diagnosed with salmonella poisoning that had triggered, through a freak immune reaction, an attack of acute pancreatitis which in turn had released enzymes into my system that were literally eating away my insides and vital organs. Initially, I was swollen with fluid, bloated to a state almost beyond recognition, but later I would lose nearly eighty pounds in weight, dwindling to the skeletal frame of someone near death. My eyes and skin became jaundiced and yellow, my body was scabby and unbearably itchy, and I was so weak I could hardly walk or even move without pain. I remember being drugged with painkillers like morphine and losing my grip on reality as horrific images filled my consciousness and I was rocked by hideous hallucinations and assaults upon my mind.

As my incredibly brave and prayerful wife Ruth looked on, I struggled with so many deep and bewildered emotions. I was aware of my three young sons, all under nine at the time, watching the deterioration of their father and wondering if I would live to see them grow into adults. I considered that my wife could suddenly become a widow in her mid-thirties. In my isolation room, I felt my life was effectively over and I felt cheated that my destiny had so suddenly been robbed from me. All the spoken promises and prophecies over my life that were ready to be fulfilled, lay like moth-eaten rags at my bed-ridden feet.

Nothing made sense. Although I can say I felt the Lord was with me in profound ways in that dark valley, I had no peace and did not know what I had done to deserve such an early death. I was helpless to do anything and too hopeless at times to rejoice in the trial. Too weak to read the Bible, I would have others read it to me whilst hanging on desperately to some precious promises recorded in Psalm 91. I remember one thing I did say to Ruth, as I observed her distress, which was something I had once heard RT Kendall say concerning how to react to all of our sufferings: "Dignify the trial! Honour God!" I believed this and meant it.

We both set our minds and wills to doing exactly this, although I can't say we found it an easy task. It was during this time that God spoke to our dear friend Terry Virgo who sent a card containing a timely message for me. The Lord had indicated to him in prayer that I was Jonah! "Wait and see!" the message said. "You will live again ... and emerge from the grave and the experience of being buried alive in the fish's belly ... to be restored to your wife and family, and your ministry. The best years of your life are yet to come." All of which seemed most unlikely.

At the same time the doctors were solemnly informing my wife that my chances of pulling through were virtually nil. Who would we believe? Well, we believed God and eventually I was "vomited out", not three days but five months later, to be miraculously restored to my family, my ministry and my church. Now, some twenty-two years on, I find myself in London, possibly one of the world's great Nineveh-like cities of our day!

The meaning of the fish

The belly of the fish is where we are reduced to nothing, or very nearly nothing. It is not ordained for us to go there so that our lives will be crippled, but divinely arranged as the place where our lives are about to be fulfilled. It is not for a diminished life but an augmented life. There may be experiences of loss in the depths, but this is only so that God can replace what has needed to be killed with fresh resources from His generous heart. Circumstances that cause us to lose our reputation, personal preferences, prejudices, biases and judgements are both executed by God and then replaced with their opposites by His care. Every day, pastors, preachers, churches, movements, institutions and major ministries are being faced with their great fish, the Father's "sentence of death" upon inadequate attitudes and human resources. And if you are really fortunate it could happen to you.

Remember that God knows best what to do with your life, and when the storm comes, you will be required to face it and submit to His loving care in the process of unfolding that often unwelcome but necessary death. It is only then that you will know the freedom of entering your true destiny. God wants to have special dealings with you in a special place. You could call it time out in "The Fish Hotel." It may last a day, three days, a week, months or even years, but I guarantee that you will never be the same person coming out of that experience as you were going into it.

Jonah's decommissioning (Jonah 2:7-9)

At the beginning of this narrative, Jonah did not care a jot about the call of God. He had heard the call to be launched on a mission to Nineveh loud and clear and had chosen to completely ignore it. To go there was too costly, grossly inconvenient and much too complex. An alternative and more easy life beckoned and Jonah gladly skipped there. Effectively, he had dropped out, gone absent without leave, washing his hands of the whole sorry saga.

In addition, Jonah was devoid of any compassion for the state of the vast population of the city of Nineveh. God was angry at their behaviour, yes, but He was also full of compassion for them. Jonah would not allow himself to lean into and be changed by that same love and kindness and God was not at all pleased about that. So Jonah was decommissioned. God was ready to face the prophet with the truth of his callous heart by arresting him violently in his tracks and dangling him over the pit of hell for a while.

Some unbelievers are given a glimpse of heaven before they go to hell. But some Christians are given a taste of hell before going to heaven. Just like Jonah, some Christians need to be faced with the reality of what God's judgement of hell truly feels like if they are ever going to be used to preach the gospel effectively enough for others to escape it. Sometimes, to look death in the face for a sustained length of time can help us defeat our fear of it.

God does not want us to be indifferent to the lost. He wants us to love them as He does. When we crowd out our lives with our own agendas, when we tenaciously hold onto things we should have relinquished, when we have paid lip service to God but not heart service, and when we have been bare-faced rebellious against God's plain directives, He will deal with us in isolation so that, with Jonah, we cry out from the place of death in order that we and others may live again. When that broadcast goes off the air, the money dries up, church members drift away, the pastor resigns, and your ministry seems to be over – it's usually then that God is getting ready to arrange a resurrection!

Thank God that with Him the stay in "The Fish Hotel" is short. He only leaves us there for as long as it takes to get us ready. Maybe today is the beginning of the end for you, and before you know it there will be a new beginning. If you are feeling lost and at sea, let me encourage you in this: *God knows exactly where you are, and when you are ready, He will come and fetch you.*

9. Jonah's Second Chance

(Jonah 2:10-3:10)

The story of Jonah is not for the fainthearted. In four short chapters, the reader is taken on an exhilarating journey through a ferocious storm, propelled to the bottom of the sea, given a front row seat as a spectator to the tragic death of God's prophet, seeing him swallowed and squashed into the confines of a fish's belly, then resurrected from the dead and ultimately baked in the oppressive heat of a searing desert. So far, we have joined Jonah on his route to Tarshish, only to be arrested by the sobering thought, "Can we ever run away from God?" The answer is, *we can try!*

Jonah tried very hard to do just that. He had decided the call of God was not for him and he was not about to start sticking his neck out for a mission he didn't want. He had paid his fare, nestling himself deep down in the hold of the ship, setting sail westwards as far away from God as he could get. There is no doubt that Jonah comes across as a miserable and nasty little man, once used to being a popular prophet and wholly resistant to any change of status in that regard. To go to Nineveh and proclaim the word of God would mean gross unpopularity and possibly mortal danger. Obeying God was all very well when there were benefits; this particular call was one he could do without.

The good news is that God knows how to deal with nasty little men. Here in chapter 3 everything changes: God takes full charge of the situation, rewinding and then reversing the plot and reissuing His original call to Jonah. After having been decommissioned by God, the prophet is given a second chance to do the right thing by turning east to face Nineveh, possibly the biggest about-turn in the Bible. From the belly of the great fish, Jonah's prayer rang out:

"I called out to the Lord, out of my distress, and He answered me; out of the belly of Sheol I cried, and You heard my voice. For You cast me into the deep, into the heart of the seas, and the flood surrounded me; all Your waves and Your billows passed over me. Then I said, 'I am driven away from your sight; yet I shall again look upon Your holy temple.' The waters closed in over me to take my life; the deep surrounded me; weeds were wrapped about my head at the roots of the mountains. I went down to the land whose bars closed upon me forever; yet You brought up my life from the pit, O Lord my God. When my life was fainting away, I remembered the Lord, and my prayer came to You, into Your holy temple. Those who pay regard to vain idols forsake their hope of steadfast love. But I with the voice of thanksgiving will sacrifice to You; what I have vowed I will pay. Salvation belongs to the Lord!" (Jonah 2:1-9)

In making the choice to run away, Jonah had given way to idolatry, setting up a false deity to guide his life's agenda and fulfil his dreams, thus forfeiting God's grace in the process. This prayer is the pivotal moment when he submits to God again, and God who hears him commands the fish to vomit Jonah onto dry land.

The transaction is made. Jonah is back on the right track and can now be given a second chance.

Jonah's recommissioning (Jonah 3:1-2)

"Then the word of the Lord came to Jonah the second time, saying, 'Arise, go to Nineveh, that great city, and call out against it the message that I tell you.'"

So the man on the run is making a surprising come back. The man who had received the call of God and rejected it, gets called a second time. The man who wanted to get as far away as possible form the city of Nineveh is again being asked to go there. The man who decided to keep his mouth shut has now decided to open it. The man who denied the message he was given from heaven is now going to deliver it as faithfully as he can. After all Jonah has done, isn't it amazing that God has decided against a dishonourable discharge and in favour of a recommission? Isn't it a relief that God's focus is not upon humiliating Jonah but focused on extending grace and forgiveness to him? He is indeed the God of second chances! Not only was Jonah given a second chance, but Nineveh was also to be given its only chance to cheat death and live again in an unprecedented day of revival ignited through the words of the prophet.

Revival times

When we pray for revival in a village, town, city or nation, what are we really praying for? Do we have only vague ideas that God will "take over" somehow and people will suddenly become Christians without encountering the message of the Gospel? Do we just sit back and let it happen? No! When we pray for revival, what we are actually praying for is for God to touch people's lives through the anointed words of the preacher. God wants to raise up men and women who will proclaim His truth fearlessly and with compassion, so that there will be a floodlight of clarity and truth shining into the lies and darkness that permeate His world. In Romans, the Apostle Paul writes,

"How then will they call on Him in whom they have not believed? And how are they to believe in Him of whom they have never heard? And how are they to hear without someone preaching? And how are they to preach unless they are sent? As it is written, 'How beautiful are the feet of those who preach the good news!'" (Romans 10:14-15)

Historically, every revival in history has been preceded by a move of God to raise up powerful preachers. In sixteenth century Europe, men such as Luther, Calvin and Knox were positioned by God to speak to every echelon of society. In the early eighteenth century when depravity was at its height, God called Whitfield, Wesley and Edwards to preach the gospel for decades on both sides of the Atlantic. Everywhere these men went, spiritual fires broke out in the hardest and most deprived communities, turning them around from their spiritual deadness into places of blessing and fruitfulness as people encountered the God of the Bible.

There is no doubt that as a result of their preaching, our nation was saved from a violent and bloody revolution, as was experienced by France in the late eighteenth century, when half of the French aristocracy lost their lives in that murderous revolution. In the nineteenth century, Charles Finney in the United States of America and William Booth and Charles Spurgeon in the United Kingdom were key preachers in a new wave of God's interaction with His people. The twentieth century has seen giants of the faith such as Billy Graham, Luis Palau and Reinhard Bonnke preach the gospel to millions all over the world.

We must pray for revival preachers!

Jonah was one such preacher. He may have blown it and ended up as "fish bait" in a sea monster at the bottom of the sea, isolated and in exile, but when he cried out in repentance, God commanded the fish to vomit him up onto dry land where He spoke to Jonah a second time. This was not just a resuscitation, it was a complete resurrection.

Good news

When we have backslidden and sunk low into a place of hiding from God, in the mire of moral failure and sin, God continues to unfold His plans for our lives. Scripture is packed full of second chances, whether it is the adulterous king David or the vain super-hero and lustful deliverer Samson, the cunning cheat Jacob or the fickle turn-coat fisherman Peter. God was faithful to His call on every one of these lives. The same is true for you and me. Have you ever thought that you had lost all trace of your influence and ministry for God, only to find that eventually God gave it back to you again some time later?

There is, however, as we see from the Jonah account, a requirement to recognise, acknowledge and repent of the sin that has entangled us, submitting ourselves both to God and to the leaders he has placed around us to help us regain the ground we have lost. Perhaps you are reading this convinced that you will never again enjoy the freedom in God that you once did due to your sin and rebellion. There is good news for you! You can.

But first, it may mean that you have to realise afresh two things you may not have clearly understood. First, the fact that this was not *your* ministry, it was *His*, to do with as He wants. Second, that It's not just *His* ministry but *yours*, and God only reluctantly ever takes it from us due to very good reasons that render this loss essential in order to avoid harm to yourself, or to others, until that danger is eliminated, and he can trust and use you once again.

God is the God of second chances!

Over the years, numbers of high profile leaders have compromised their morality and reputation in various ways.

Leaders such as Gordon MacDonald and Jim Bakker come to mind. In Gordon MacDonald's case, a one-off extra-marital sexual liaison during a period of depression and vulnerability became household news across the USA, and then the world, due to his former integrity and high profile influence. The news networks picked it up as a scoop and a media feeding frenzy began. MacDonald's response to his sin was the opposite of so many: he did not defend himself or his actions, or rebel against any measures needed to restore him, but submitted himself wholeheartedly to the pastors and leaders entrusted with his rehabilitation process. In time, he not only recovered his relationship with the Lord and his loved ones, but also his remarkable ministry. He went on to write *Ordering Your Private World* which became a bestseller, highlighting the importance of the pursuit of internal holiness over external religious behaviour.

Jim Bakker, with his wife Tammy Faye, were, in the 1980's, at the helm of the well known American network, PTL Ministries, a huge charismatic evangelical empire including a theme park which generated millions of dollars every year to fund outreach campaigns. As Jim Bakker and his colleagues would admit, once the numbers reached this level, all they could do was keep the machine running, which meant they lost sight of God. Eventually, Jim and Tammy Faye were exposed for their double-dealing and fraud and Jim received a substantial jail term. While in prison, he was given a book by RT Kendall, *God Meant it for Good*, which outlines the story of Joseph and his exposure to danger, loss, and his darkest days at the hands of his envious brothers, leading to his long-term betrayal and false imprisonment.

Jim Bakker encountered God afresh while reading this book in his prison cell and gave his life back to Christ, fully repenting of his dishonesty and failure. On his release from incarceration, and in a radical departure from his previous life of big money and high profile, he went back to his roots to set up a little known work amongst drug addicts in the inner city.

These testimonies are included here to give glory to the One who resurrects lives that have lost their way, lifting them from the depths of darkness and back into the light. No one can save their ministry if God has arranged they should lose it. But then, no one can permanently lose their ministry if God has ordained they recover it. God will make sure that they get it back. Every conversion is a new beginning, including the conversion of the prophet Jonah. He may have been nothing more than fish bait and fish vomit, but God never gave up on him. After three days in death, Jonah is raised up once again, ready to hear the voice of God once more.

The essence of effective ministry

Any future role that Jonah would have in Nineveh was reliant on the word of the Lord. He would not be able to function without it. The essence of a ministry that affects lives for the better, possibly changing the spiritual atmosphere of cities and nations, is ultimately dependent on God's voice. What else can we move out on? What else could Jonah have done? If God had simply commanded the fish to vomit Jonah onto dry land and then left him, what would or could Jonah have done relying on his own initiative and resources alone? How effective would he have been? That God's word came a second time to Jonah is a sign of His immense grace and commitment. It is evidence of what our forefathers in the faith called "the perseverance of the saints" or, more accurately, "the preservation of the saints" – since God's part in this is far more important than our efforts in responding to His grace. Not only that, it is an example to us of the amazing privileges we have as children of God. Jonah forfeited, "the grace that could have been his" (Jonah 2:8b), but God re-commissioned him so that Jonah not only *knew* what he had been saved *from*, but *what* he had been saved *for*.

All of a sudden his life was restored to its original purpose and the light flooded in. Jonah had been saved from the acidic insides of a fish belly for the hot desert sands of Assyria. There were thousands of people in Nineveh in desperate need for the voice of God to split the darkness, and Jonah was the only prophet God had chosen and wanted to help Him achieve this miracle.

You have not "lost it"

Do you know what you have been saved *from*, and do you know what you have been saved *for*? Do you feel like you have lost your gifting, calling or ministry somewhere in the depths of a dark ocean? Was this once your plight, but you can bear witness to the grace of God who has given it back to you again sometime later?

There are two encouragements from the book of Jonah to help us through our Christian life and ministry, often pursued amidst great difficulties:

1. Your ministry is on loan

Your ministry skills, gifts, talents and anointing do not belong to you, they belong to God. It is He who ministers through you, in connection with you relationship with Himself, for the benefit of His Church and His world. God can take away a ministry any time He wants to, and He often does. I have known countless preachers, teachers and leaders, widely known to many and highly effective who suddenly found themselves "all at sea". In many cases they have done nothing wrong; they have not run off with church funds or had numerous sordid affairs, but everything has just shut down for them. Where they used to hear from God, He is silent. Where they would once preach and see people receive Christ, their words fall on deaf ears. Some have said to me, "I don't know what God is doing in my life, but He seems to have forgotten me. I am now shelved, apparently even out of God's reach and covered in cobwebs and dust." God can and will take us to places where our busyness ends and our solitude has begun. He does this to clean us out, realign our focus and remind us that we are who we are because of His grace and His grace alone. As we relinquish our pride, He calls us a second time, restoring our hope, our joy, and our passion for His ways.

2. Your ministry is for keeps

Here is the paradox. Although God will take away a ministry for a season, He does not like doing it without the hope of restoration. You do not have to fight to keep the gifts God originally gave to you. In effect, you are in His control and like a weaned child on its mother's knee you learn to trust that God knows what He is doing (Psalm 131). God will never forsake you. He will make sure that what has been stolen from you will be returned to you. If He wants you to walk in a particular calling, He will preserve you, your walk, and your calling, so that after your time in the belly of the fish is over, you can enter into His fullness once again. He has not destined you to limp through life filled with regret but to dance through life with frequent strong measures of joy. Whatever else, He will keep you on track and He never walks away from us personally when we fail. The book of Proverbs states, "For the righteous falls seven times and rises again" (Proverbs 24:16a). So with God, we can always retrace our steps to where we missed our way, and get back on track with the Lord.

Have you taken a detour? Has it been weeks, months or years? Do you feel you have mislaid something vital and precious? Have you known God's call on your life and He has put it on hold for reasons you can't explain?

Nothing is more important than life with God. The graphic account of the catastrophic disorder that swirls around Jonah as he runs away from God is a clear indication of how it feels for us when we move away from the centre of His will. Maybe it is time to go back to where you once were in your relationship with your God. You may well find that He wants to speak with you again.

Where did you lose it?

The exact location of Jonah's expulsion from the big fish is unclear. Some say he was taken all around the coast of Africa only to be deposited in the Persian Gulf to ease his journey to Nineveh. More likely is that he was simply brought back to Joppa, from where he had first boarded the ship. Sometimes, God insists we we retrace our steps. We may take a circuitous route back to God, or it may be more direct, but what is most important is that we go back and reclaim what we have lost.

In the Old Testament we read about how Elisha ran a School of Prophets. In 2 Kings 6:1-7 there is an account of the building of a new accommodation block to house the trainee prophets. One man had borrowed an axe from a friend to cut trees to provide timber for their dwellings. In the course of using it, the axe head flew off and landed in the muddy River Jordan, sinking deep into the murky depths. In a state of high anxiety, the man approaches Elisha with the news that the borrowed axe head was lost. Elisha asks the man, "Where did you lose it?", and the man shows him the exact place. Elisha simply throws a stick into the river and, miraculously, the heavy iron axe head appears on the surface of the water. At this point, we could say that the careless trainee prophet recovered his cutting edge!

If you and I are to recover our cutting edge, the principles of recovery are timeless in this story from 2 Kings 6. We have to honestly own up to and admit our responsibility for losing it. Then acknowledge its not our personal property to dispose of in whatever way we like, it is on loan to us. We then need to retrace our steps to the exact place and circumstances in which we discarded or lost it. Then seek the help God alone can give to find and restore it once again. Our final privilege is to reach out our hand personally to retrieve and reclaim it and then use it as God directs us. God may therefore ask you the same question more than once: "Where did you lose it?" Whilst it may be uncomfortable to answer Him, it is our God-given opportunity to experience and signal a very personal miracle. It is at this point that we are faced with a second chance so that all that was lost has the possibility of coming back to us. Amazingly, God is like that. He is in the recovery and recycling business.

Jonah was given a second chance and Nineveh thus had her second chance also. Both the prophet and the city were offered a lifeline. God is the God of unending grace and mercy and He will do all that He can to save you for what He made and destined you for. What a privilege to be loved, cared for, and protected by a God such as this.

10. Jonah's Great Revival

(Jonah 3:1-10)

Apparently Jonah experienced the wonderful privilege of being called by God not just once but twice. That God had initially given the prophet his mission to Nineveh was an example of His grace to the city. But the fact that Jonah was also called again, after so brazenly ignoring it the first time, shows both God's total commitment to His word and His unwavering commitment to His people. God does not desire the death of the wicked and will literally move heaven and earth to offer His loved ones a second chance. This was good news for Jonah, good news for Nineveh, and it is good news for us.

In chapter 2 verse 10 God commanded the fish to vomit out the contents of its stomach onto dry land. When God's time has come, our time has come. When God's time has not come, our time has not come. But God's time had come for Jonah, signalled by a command from God that marked the moment that the great sea-monster would vomit resurrected Jonah onto dry land again.

Not only was it unusual for a huge sea creature to swim to the shallows to do this, at the risk of being beached and stranded, but the contents of its stomach were also abnormal: a fully-grown man! Jonah was unceremoniously expelled by the fish at the request of God and in response to his penitence from the depths of Sheol where he finally promised to do what he had been called to do. Jonah would go to Nineveh to tell them the truth, the whole truth and nothing but the truth – the great truth that salvation belonged only to the Lord.

Without wishing to appear tasteless, the process of vomiting usually occurs when the body experiences one of the following:

• Something harmful has been swallowed which the body recognises as a foreign substance or object

• Too much food has been consumed which the body is unable to digest

• As an involuntary response, triggered by the sight or sound of something sickening

• After a physical blow to the stomach

God had given the swollen belly of the big fish one almighty commanding punch so that the contents were propelled onto the land, ready to be addressed by God a second time. Something powerful needed to happen to release Jonah from his hideous inescapable hideout and back onto the road to Nineveh and to judgement or salvation for its people. Perhaps all four causes were deployed.

If God will do this for Jonah, He will do it for you and me. It may be unpleasant at times, but it is far better than remaining inanimate in the belly of darkness. When God gives us a second chance, it marks the beginning of new hope and a fresh start – not just for our lives, but also for the lives of those around us.

Time to speak out

After three full days of silence in the place of slimy and stinking death, where Jonah could neither hear God nor speak His word, the time had come for an awakening. For a city or nation to be offered hope and experience true revival, two conditions are necessary.

1. The presence of a man or woman of God who have made themselves available to God
2. An authentic word from God relayed by that man or woman to God's chosen recipients

Unless a word comes from God, a particular situation will not simply change automatically. You won't change, your church won't change, your town or city won't change. The city of Nineveh was in perpetual darkness because the light of God's word had not yet reached it. We know this was the case, as Jonah had not made himself fully available as the man of God he was. Until the word was delivered to that city, the people were decaying in the deathly silence of a void.

This is the most terrible famine of all, and as in a physical famine, the young will always suffer the worst from the unbelief of their guides, teachers and mentors (Amos 8:11-13).

Christianity is the only enterprise in the world that expands primarily through the agency of preaching. In the babble of human philosophies and confused ideologies, our world is desperate for the beautiful message of salvation, spoken out in truth, love and clarity by chosen men and women of God. If people do not hear it, how will they believe it?

It is no wonder that Satan wants to silence preachers, deterring them from answering the call of God or luring them away when they have heard it. Where there is no preaching there is no progress, and it is vital we take a stand against any demonic strategy to mute the preacher or preaching of God's word.

So Jonah now had the word and this time it was slightly different from before. When God gave the initial call, the prophet was told,

"Go to the great city of Nineveh and preach against it, because its wickedness has come up before Me." (Jonah 1:2 NIV)

But when the second call was given, God said,

"Go to the great city of Nineveh and proclaim to it the message I give you." (Jonah 3:2 NIV)

Notice that there is a shift in mood.

God's righteous anger in the first example has softened by the second, indicating that in His grace, God has plans for a surprisingly positive outcome for Nineveh. No longer was Jonah to preach against the city but rather *to it*.

Nineveh's great revival

The greatest miracle in the Jonah narrative is not the violent storm that came at just the right time, nor is it the presence of a vulturous great fish or even the spectacular resurrection of a prophet. Rather, it is the definitive repentance of the people of Nineveh. There is no doubt that the conversion of a single soul is a great miracle, but the awakening of a lawless, depraved, idolatrous, immoral city *en masse* is utterly breathtaking.

The account in chapter three puts it quite simply thus: "And the people of Nineveh believed God" (Jonah 3:5a). The process by which this Assyrian city renounced its evil ways and embraced the ways of God can be traced in three steps.

1. The Message

On reaching Nineveh, a city that took three days to cross on foot, Jonah delivered an unadorned, straightforward message of judgement whenever and wherever he could.

"Yet forty days, and Nineveh shall be overthrown!" (Jonah 3:4b)

The word had finally come after its long detour and it was not particularly positive. The biblical narrative is stark, and as we read it we can imagine Jonah, grim faced with a hostile demeanour similar to the joyless zealots depicted in contemporary cartoon characterisations of gaunt, bearded street preachers, wearing sandwich boards emblazoned with the gloomy message, *The End Is Nigh!*

Who would stop to listen to it? Who stops to listen to God's warnings today? Very few want to hear Heaven's views on the issues of homosexuality, abortion, violence, pride, adultery and greed. Defending the biblical position on these and other matters central to human welfare, can lead to arrest and unwelcome hostile media exposure. The irony is often that those who speak out the truths of Scripture are often subsequently taken to court and required to swear on the same Bible in order to defend charges against a subversive position that is being arraigned as criminal activity, yet it derives its origin from that very same Bible.

Jonah preached an urgent eschatological message to the people of Nineveh. He was proclaiming the message of God regarding the "end times" for this city that had soaked itself in the polluted cesspit of sin and debauchery, and now stunk to high heaven. The reality of its coming judgement was real and, in forty days time, there would be nothing left of this immoral place but a sticky stain on the desert floor. In fact, Nineveh had already experienced a warning some years previously, but a renewed sense of urgency was to be conveyed. Life is not only to be lived for today, but with a conscious awareness of tomorrow. Nineveh's time was fast running out.

Records show that on June 15th 763BC there was a complete solar eclipse over this area of Assyria, and devastating floods and famine had followed. As the ancient world had no clear understanding of the workings of the cosmos, an eclipse would have been a truly ominous event, which announced the anger of the gods. Perhaps this was, after all, Nineveh's second warning, her second chance to repent. Had God already softened her to ready the capital for the visitation of the prophet Jonah?

We can never know.

But we can be sure of this: God wanted Nineveh to consider her demise and He wants us to soberly do the same today in nations that have also provoked God's anger.

We will not know how to live in this world until we consider more seriously what lies beyond it. Few people are ready to receive mercy until they have experienced the reality that they are under judgement. Life is not meant to be lived as if there was no tomorrow, as pessimistic and hopeless existentialists would encourage us to do, authenticating their lives in reckless or self-destructive ways. Scripture teaches us that we have an eternal destiny and our final destination is not predetermined, at least as far as we are concerned.

We have a choice.

God will regularly shock us out of our inertia in order to face us with the fact that without Him, we are decidedly not safe.

In a world where, in the main, the preaching of the gospel has focused more on mercy than judgement, the message of the book of Jonah recalibrates our understanding of God as a God of mercy and judgement. Without an acknowledgement of His faithfulness in telling us the truth, we cannot encounter His boundless mercy to undo the same.

Unusual events

When the out of the ordinary happens it is likely that God is shaking His world so that we take notice of how far we have fallen. Over the last thirty years there have been some very unusual weather patterns across the globe, which have resulted in severe shocks and shortages of basic commodities. Tsunamis, earthquakes, hurricanes and typhoons often headline the news reports and images of devastation that proliferate on our television screens. Communities that thought they were safe are ravaged by the violence of nature unleashed, often in a matter of minutes. Families are torn apart by unstoppable waves, winds and quakes.

So too, acts of terrorism have escalated on an unprecedented scale. We are regularly told about many different barbaric acts from that of a lone gunman shooting the innocent at close range on a high school campus to religious fanatics flying aircraft into buildings, killing thousands. Whose life is immune? No one's.

Following the attacks on the Twin Towers of September 11th 2001, churches in New York and elsewhere across the USA were packed full of people who, searching their hearts, were desperate to reconnect with God – at the same time acknowledging that life was not as it should be without Him. Something had changed. This nightmare was a warning of what can happen when the world spirals into suicidal self-destruction and death. Although God did not, and never would, mastermind these attacks, they were the impetus for a loud wake-up call to admit our need of Him, and a vivid reminder of the vulnerability of any nation that turns it back upon God. Warnings such as these are often permitted by God.

This may not be the tactic you or I would adopt, but of course, we are not God. Speaking on His behalf, the prophets of the Bible regularly used to alarm people with their confrontational solemn preaching, so it was not a role for the faint-hearted. Jeremiah even objected to the content of a message he received from God, deciding to say nothing at all, only to admit later that he could not keep quiet because God's word burned inside him to the point where he confessed he could not suppress it any longer. Have you ever had a case of spiritual heart-burn?

"If I say, 'I will not mention him, or speak any more in His name,' there is in my heart as it were a burning fire shut up in my bones, and I am weary with holding it in, and I cannot." (Jeremiah 20:9)

Jesus would sometimes scare people with His messages, especially when He taught on hell, which He did more than any other writer or speaker in the Old or New Testaments. So too, preachers through the ages from the apostle Paul to George Whitfield, John Wesley to William Booth, would state very clearly the effects and dangerous outcomes of a life without God.

Jonathan Edwards saw the whole town of Northampton, Massachusetts awaken to God after years of practicing formal religion, but only after he preached a sermon entitled, "Sinners in the hands of an angry God." It is reported that when he had finished speaking, members of the congregation were literally holding onto the pillars of the church for fear they would be swallowed up by the ground opening up beneath them and sink into hell. The whole town wept through the night as people fell under the conviction of the Holy Spirit. Only the Church of Jesus Christ can sound the bell of truth so clearly that people awaken to the reality that He is the only answer to the biggest questions of life and of death!

Urgent times

Jonah was direct and unrelenting in his message to the Ninevites in declaring that they had no longer than forty days of existence remaining. As far as he understood it, God's judgement would fall and the people, houses, temples, crops and animals would all be annihilated approximately six weeks hence. Jonah would have appeared from nowhere, possibly still stained and covered in vomit and seaweed, bearing the fresh scars of acid burns from the belly of the fish and even perhaps smelling of death. This was no fresh-faced, jovial foreigner, happy to be on a sightseeing trip to the ancient near-Middle East! The prophet of God carried the marks of his own encounter with a God whose wrath whipped up a storm around him, plunging him into death. He was a living, breathing sign of what God would do with errant sinners. Jonah delivered God's message to a city about to encounter what he himself had lived through and it was this that measured his credibility, as the message weighed heavily in the sultry air of the streets of Nineveh. The urgency of this announcement would have been unmistakable. As one preacher observed, "The truths a man has got from the Bible and verified in his own experience is the real measure of his power."

   Sin is abhorrent to God. He is not passive, indifferent or lazy in His plans to eliminate it, and when He comes to deal with it, there will be nowhere to hide. Time was running out for Nineveh and no longer were they going to get away with their pursuit of evil, for in forty days God would sweep in and destroy them. Jonah's message was not complex or difficult to understand – just eight words in most Bibles – and you don't need to consult a dictionary for the meaning of any of these words:

"Forty more days and Nineveh will be overturned."

Less than 1000 hours were left for Nineveh to remain alive, and Jonah looked and sounded like he meant it. He'd been sent, he'd been sunk, he'd been saved, and now he'd been sent a second time. Nineveh believed him. You would probably have believed him too.

If God is not ambivalent concerning sin, as Christians we should adopt the same attitude. It is a pity that in general, the body of Christ seems to have lost its determination to prioritise purity and reject ambiguity. The choices made by some radical unbelievers in society have seeped through the walls of our churches and diluted the message of Christ who came to rid the world of sin. Our cities, towns and places of worship are no longer guaranteed to be relatively sin-free zones though we spend thousands of pounds on child protection policies and security cameras. We take precautions, and rightly so, to protect our people from the infiltration of evil, assuming nothing is safe. What a world we live in! We see unborn babies as our personal property and dispose of them as an inconvenience. Children are forced into horrendous situations of abuse and neglect at the whim of the sexually depraved. Drugs and alcohol are considered a right, and are easily available from the pusher looking to get rich quick. The god of money and materialism is worshipped as we continue to spend more than we have, whilst watching economies everywhere spiralling out of control.

We live in desperate times!

There is a sense of urgency upon us to align ourselves with the One who created His world and "...saw that it was good" (Genesis 1:10b). If a bearded, unkempt prophet stood in front of Parliament today announcing the demise of London in six weeks time, would you listen? Would anyone listen? Probably not.

Furthermore, if God asked you to carry the same message to your town or city or nation, would you obey? For those of us who are passionate about God and long to see Him break into the moral decay of our toxic society, we have a challenge to cease caring about whether or not we are liked, loved, accepted or wanted by the people to whom we speak.

Like Jonah, our primary responsibility is to fear God more than we fear people. The times we live in are indeed urgent times.

2. The Destination

In a sprawling city full of people from all walks of life, it is possible to become easily lost. Cities can be the loneliest places on earth for the simple reason that there is increased access to covert sin and it is less likely you will be found out if you participate in it. People come and go in the busyness of life, not stopping to watch those around them in their pursuit of their own pleasures and success. We can even guard our own anonymity as we do the same things.

Cities are important to God and they should be important to us. I am glad that God cares about the city of London in which I currently live, because I feel a call to it and I feel His heart for it. How glad I am that God called me to this work and not to the rolling fields of the countryside! The countryside has millions of trees, and they are beautiful. But cities have millions of people, and God loves people more than he loves trees. That's why we should love the city more than we love the countryside. I do not simply live here for my own agenda, but to follow the call of God. Sin may be prolific in my city, but so is the potential for detoxification and decontamination through the gospel of Jesus Christ, and God is at work in our land, in its cities, awakening people to His presence.

Jonah was called to a city of 140,000 people and God still wants volunteers who will answer the call to the great cities of our world today. Will you answer His call? Remember the testimonies of the great preachers sent to speak to the great cities of our nation in years gone by. John Knox, for instance, preached with such power in Edinburgh that it was said his monarch, Queen Mary, feared his preaching more than an army of five thousand invaders. Just one man! William Booth preached to thousands on the streets of London along with his Salvation Army officers, boldly addressing the most hostile and difficult audiences who pelted them with faeces and rotten garbage, yet they were totally fearless in the face of threats and violence. Because He cares about people, God will raise up men and women today who will proclaim His truth in the darkest places and activate repentance and change in the spiritual atmosphere, street by street if necessary.

3. The Result

The greatest miracle and sign of all is *conversion*. Whilst I honour the presence and reality of all the five-fold ministries of Ephesians 4:11 still operating in the Church and in the world today, I believe the greatest of them is the evangelist. I both admire this anointing and long to grow in it. When I see an evangelist at work, I am deeply encouraged and inspired by the fire in their belly and their passion to see lost souls saved. I catch something of their ability to draw people into a revelation of the love of God and rejoice with them as they lead others to Christ so effectively. They help people to see that they are far worse than they thought they were, but also to see that God is far more gracious than they thought He was.

In Nineveh, the results of Jonah's prophetic warning were remarkable. He walked into an un-evangelized zone and the narrative tells us that the people simply awoke from their stupour and accepted the message! Let us notice some outstanding features of the process by which that city turned back to God.

• *It began with them believing God* (Jonah 3:5a). They may have had many systems of belief prior to Jonah's visit, but they were nearly all in error. Dangerous ideas, false claims, lies and idolatry had filtered into every strata of Nineveh's society, corrupting it from the inside out. Where Assyrian myths once filled their minds, now they believed the truth about God. As Jonah spoke, the scales fell from their eyes and they encountered the miracle of heaven's revelation of truth. The prophet was simply an instrument in God's hands to bring about this complete change of mind, as this was not a fleshly tactic of persuasion, but a spiritual transaction of faith.

• *It issued in repentance* (Jonah 3:5-6). The true meaning of repentance is not just saying sorry, it is coming to the realization that we have offended God and turning around to think again about our life and relationship with Him. It is a "putting off" of the old and a "putting on" of the new. When repentance occurs, God appears so dazzlingly holy and we appear so desperately sinful that we lose hope of ever being saved at all. That is what happened in Nineveh and it was reflected in the change of clothing across the whole of the city, from smooth silks to itchy sackcloth. Whereas man without God elevates his own self-image, man with God can only elevate God's divine image as the norm for humanity. From the account in Jonah we see a change of clothes coming from a change of heart.

• *It was a visible response* (Jonah 3:5-6). When revival happens, it is impossible to hide it. Word spreads as the media reports it and crowds are drawn to it. There was nothing more visible than the king of Nineveh replacing his fine apparel with rough sackcloth. During the times of revival in Pensacola, Florida in the mid 1990's, one million people passed through one single church to hear the gospel preached and see for themselves what was happening. Thousands of people came to faith in Christ at that time, stunned by the presence of the Holy Spirit operating in such an unusual way.

• *It was a universal response* (Jonah 3:5). The narrative tells us that a fast from food was declared and all of the people, from the greatest to the least, were a part of it. It would have involved all ages, from babies to the elderly. It would have touched "fat cat" businessmen and those below the poverty line, the dignified and undignified. The gospel is a great leveller which ends celebrity and status seeking and instead, focusing on the hearts, minds and wills of men, women and children alike. God becomes the main attraction in the process of repentance as He takes our fallen flesh and the battle with self, and crushes it under His feet, releasing a person into a restored relationship with their God. We want God more than we want our daily food.

• *It was a public response* (Jonah 3:7b). Modelled first by the Assyrian king, who not only heard Jonah's message but preached it too, so the Ninevites were told what their response should be. He issued a decree, recorded here in perfect Hebrew, that there would be a universal fast and that everyone including the animals should wear sackcloth. John Wesley once said, "When a man gets converted, even his dog should know it!" If animals are affected by the mood of human beings (as seems to be the general opinion of the experts on the Hebrew of verse 8), perhaps it seems fitting that the animals of Nineveh shared in their owners' sorrow. Imagine a monarch or president or prime minister issuing this type of decree today! This was true revival in Nineveh and our hearts must begin to ache for the same corporate and public sorrow today.

• *It led to life-changing actions* (Jonah 3:8). Nineveh was the world centre of violence, focused on the acquisition of plunder, aggressive conquest, idolatry and self-centredness. However, their repentance led in turn to works of repentance, specifically the abandonment of false gods and idols, violence, cruelty and aggression. What counts for much in this world often counts for nothing in the next world. Revival helps us evaluate things properly. Their hearts were changed and their values came to match the values held by God. Somehow they knew what was right. This is so often the testimony of those who have become Christians, whose lives are suddenly turned around and their behaviour becomes the very opposite of what it had been previously.

• *It involved a deep humility and desperation before God* (Jonah 3:8-9). The people of Nineveh, led by the king, appealed to God for pardon and mercy. It is not our born right to receive mercy, just as it was not the born right of the people of Nineveh, but in His grace God withholds that which we justly deserve and in His loving-kindness gives us that which we do not, nor could ever, deserve, namely, His forgiveness – all for the sake of Christ who came at the mid-point of history to open the flood gates of God's mercy for us all. *And God's response?*

"When God saw what they did, how they turned from their evil ways, God relented of the disaster that He had said He would do to them, and He did not do it." (Jonah 3:10)

Amazingly, when man repents, God repents. Whatever God had justly planned for the city of Nineveh now melted away In response to the humility and sincere repentance and remorse of the people. The Psalmist writes that,

"The Lord is merciful and gracious, slow to anger and abounding in steadfast love." (Psalm 103:8 ESV)

So He changed His mind about Nineveh's fate.

Maybe it is time for the word of the Lord to come to us "a second time". Let us pray that we shall also see Him relent and change His mind over the fate of our nation, as we drench both our church auditoriums and our town pavements with our tears of shame and repentance, so that God may be moved to show revival mercy to us also. After all, He is the God of outrageous grace!

Everything God did in Nineveh is just as possible where you live too. *With God, all things are possible.*

11. Jonah's Quarrel With God

(Jonah 4:1-11)

It is perhaps a little difficult for us to identify with the resonances of the word "Nineveh" in the same way as the Jews of Jonah's time might have done so. But it may help us to realise that it was rapidly becoming the capital of a world-gobbling empire, notorious for it's cruel, rapacious, ruthless and genocidal, ambitions for conquest. Not the most inviting mission field that a keen Christian believer could be summoned by God to travel on a mercy-mission to!

I called the book in your hands *The Jonah Complex* for the simple reason that, though the biblical text is well known for its brevity, it contains within it a labyrinth of intricate twists and turns. In this story we have shadowed the prophet of God in his quest to escape God's call to Nineveh, on his run to a ship and his eagerness to flee westwards, in both calm and storm, then suddenly plunged to the bottom of the sea where we joined him in the belly of the great fish, eventually finding rest on *terra firma* at an unidentified shore, then walking nervously with him into the darkness of the doomed city of Nineveh, only to witness this city unexpectedly reach out for the light of uncertain hope in the face of God's threat, clothed in itchy sackcloth and craving God's mercy.

Very few people would embrace the call of God to a city like Nineveh. To the average ancient Israelite, just the mention of its name would have made them shudder with fear. In more recent history, words like The Third Reich, Chechnya, the Killing Fields, Auschwitz, Bosnia and Afghanistan would have a similar effect on people of every background and different ages.

In some senses, however, *we are all Jonah*! God calls us to engage His world in its manifold desperate need of His touch and healing, but we have a choice as to whether we accept this mission or not. If we decide to run away, He will not give up on us that easily, pursuing us to a place where we acknowledge that it is far better to be in the centre of His will than on the edges of it. We will then perhaps be offered a second chance and, God willing, all will be well.

Or will it? The Jonah narrative does not end with a big party in Nineveh at which the prophet of God is honoured as their special guest at a banquet. In fact, there are no celebrations that involved Jonah at all. And even if there had been, he would have turned down the invitation. As the population of this penitent city came to terms with its approaching fate at the hands of a vengeful God, Jonah was preparing to set up camp outside the city walls, ready to watch it burn! He had delivered the message, closely observed the reactions to it in barely disguised disgust, and assumed that God would not relent from His strategy of destruction – probably because Jonah had said so!

However, at the end of chapter three, there is the unexpected and surprising outcome that it is not judgement but mercy that is the primary motivation in God's heart. Nineveh will not be destroyed, but will survive and become prosperous again in spite of the ominous consequences this could bring upon Israel.

Jonah's anger

"But it displeased Jonah exceedingly, and he was angry." (Jonah 4:1)

Although Jonah himself had encountered the mercy of God and had praised Him for it, ironically he was incensed when God showed the same mercy to a huge city in peril. As far as Jonah was concerned, it was inevitable that Nineveh would get everything God had threatened, and that was deservedly coming to them. His realignment to the call of God and the successful execution of the operation to announce to the Ninevites their impending annihilation had all gone very well indeed: job well done. *Now let's wait for the fireworks.*

That this prophetic time bomb was to be defused and disengaged was not part of the plan! Jonah had to face the sharp truth that God had surprisingly changed His mind, and that sudden turnaround had made the prophet very angry indeed. It was, quite frankly, outrageous! Like generations of believers after him, Jonah had been pressurised to accept that God could work in any way He wanted to, and He would not be restricted by the expectations of anyone or anything. Instead of keeping His word, God relented the destruction He had planned for Nineveh, withholding the wrath they had so richly deserved and replacing it with the surprising mercy that they manifestly did not deserve. *Outrageous!*

The missing key to the plot

"And he prayed to the Lord and said, 'O Lord, is this not what I said when I was yet in my country? This is what made me flee to Tarshish; for I knew that you are a gracious God and merciful, slow to anger and abounding in steadfast love, and relenting from disaster." (Jonah 2:2)

The narrator of Jonah is now ready to unveil the final mystery lurking behind Jonah's strange rebellion and dangerous flight from God's call and commission to preach doom to Nineveh. Without this revelation we would risk failing to understand God's extraordinary dealings with His wayward prophet, and we would also bypass or even comfortably evade the book's central message to us all, seeing this story as merely a quirky cameo of a difficult character and his personality disorder, designed for the amusement of shallow readers looking for some unusual entertainment. Few readers, to this day, end their reading of Jonah feeling even remotely disturbed, let alone forced to concede and reluctantly confess with some sense of surprise and horror that, "I am Jonah!"

The truth is, the very same man who had recently praised God for showing underserved mercy and sudden deliverance to himself (see 2:1-9), has all along resented the very possibility of this happening as the final outcome for Nineveh. And so, just as Jonah had suspected from the start, some time not far into the forty days delay before God's destruction was meted out upon the hapless and helpless doomed residents of Nineveh, God changed His mind!

We discover that Jonah had suspected that this was what would happen all along, and that this suspicion was the fundamental reason for his rebellious protest and sudden flight westwards on the kind of transport "landlubber" poor sailors like the Israelites of that time would have normally avoided like the plague! But for Jonah it was better to risk death at sea due to his dereliction of duty to God, than risk God showing favour to those "damned undeserving heathen" who needed to be wiped off the map before they could do any more damage to anyone, ever again!

The words "mercy", "clemency" and "pardon" in Jonah's vocabulary should only be reserved for himself and his fellow Israelites. And this deep secret is the key to the plot. It unlocks the real significance of God's original intention in sending Jonah, and also Jonah's stubborn resignation from his life calling, eventually leading to the awesome and unexpected outcome of revival for Nineveh itself. God's grace is the centrepiece of the story, and all too many mean-spirited believers fail to identify with such outrageous favour and actions on God's part. Sinners simply don't deserve this kind of "bleeding heart" soft treatment, and God must be out of His mind to be acting this way!

What kind of a God is God?

Some years ago, I read a magazine article about a notorious American serial killer called Jeffrey Dahmer who had been in prison for years, awaiting execution for his crimes. He'd been arrested and tried for the heinous crimes of viciously torturing and mutilating at least eleven kidnapped victims, resorting to necrophilia and cannibalism, and burying their mutilated body parts under his floorboards. He was completely cold and expressionless during his trial, voicing no remorse or repentance for his actions. The death penalty was deemed eminently just and appropriate. The jury and public observers hated him. The public's unanimous and shrill cry was, "Fry him!" – alluding to the electric chair he was possibly facing. His sentence, however, was finally announced to be life imprisonment without parole.

A few years into that term Dahmer was visited by Bible-toting Christians eager to give him the gospel. A series of deep encounters took place over many weeks, in which Dahmer saw for the first time the corruption of his soul through his early exposure and subsequent addiction to pornography, and the deadly path his behaviour had taken ever since. He deeply repented of his former life, then came to believe in Jesus Christ as the only one who could reverse his depravity and save him. He became an unashamed Christian, subsequently devoting countless hours to reading the Bible and many Christian books as he grew in his faith and integrity, whilst never disputing the fact that he deserved to die for his crimes. He was subsequently baptized into Christ, and close observers reported that he had started to smile again. He later went public with vocal and eloquent statements of his new perspectives upon his crimes in the sincere and strong hope of deterring others from ever repeating them by foolishly taking the same downhill path with pornography that he had once taken.

As a result, the surprising news of his conversion became widely known and vilified as a cheap shot to elicit public sympathy. The media went into a frenzy of protest and angry reports of the wide expressions of public ridicule against his profession of Christian conversion. One striking headline in the press asked in bold type, WHO IS RESPONSIBLE FOR THIS OUTRAGE? And, of course, the shocking and unexpected final answer to that question is, "God"! Surprisingly, it was actually God's idea to save Jeffrey Dahmer.

On November 28th, 1994, Dahmer and another prison inmate were beaten to death with an iron bar stolen from the prison gym, killed by a fellow-inmate. A lot of people were very glad about that. Jonah might have been quite pleased too.

The facts concerning God's surprising grace provoke another question from most people's lips: "What kind of God would do that for a person as depraved as Jeffrey Dahmer?" For this story of one of the world's worst and most cold-blooded killers and the

questions it inevitably arouses, might well cause us all to think of
the possibility that a *Jonah* may lurk somewhere in the hidden
recesses of each of our hearts. Jonah was angry at the way God
had run things – even though he acknowledges the true nature of
God in the narrative:

"...for I knew that you are a gracious God and merciful, slow
to anger and abounding in steadfast love, and relenting from
disaster." (Jonah 4:2b ESV)

Yet, Jonah was peeved that Nineveh would not get what it so
rightly deserved at God's hands. "Payback time" was indefinitely
postponed and God's goodness was such an affront to him to
the point where he could not even begin to handle it. Grace is
sometimes totally outrageous!

I have known many Christians who act in the same way. They
live their lives angry with people, angry with circumstances, angry
with missed opportunities, angry with their church leaders and
angry with God. This smouldering aggression will often lie dormant
until challenged, until such a time as this religious spirit rises up
and hits out in an explosion of frustration. This hissing pride is
manifest in all manner of ways and stands in direct opposition
to the kindness and love of God who wants all men, women and
children everywhere to be saved. No one deserves God's mercy,
but all can access and receive it. Probably, we should all feel
uncomfortable as we read this part of the Jonah account, since
it challenges our own inconsistencies in our personal appraisal of
the nature and character of the Christ we claim, and indeed aim,
to imitate.

God is not partial. He cares as much about the salvation of
the rich as He does the poor. His heart for the uneducated beats
just as strongly as it does for the most respected academics.
The octogenarian in their twilight years has as much freedom to

receive Christ as the fresh faced youth full of hope and vigour. There are no restrictions on God's mercy and love, other than those God chooses for Himself. It was not Jonah's place to be haughty and superior when it came to the destiny of Nineveh and the same is true for us today. If our pride and religious spirit keeps people away from encountering the mercy of God, He may well have something quite strong to say about it.

God's question

Jonah felt so wound up and indignant about this that he in effect he said to God, "If you let them live, then let me die!" (v.3). He wanted disaster. God gave Nineveh grace. So Jonah threw his toys out of the pram in a petulant tantrum whilst wishing he was dead himself. Dead would be better. Better nothing than something not worth having!

We've probably all resented what we think God didn't deservedly do for us and what we observe He has clearly done undeservedly for others. We have questioned God's wisdom, abilities, timing, kindness and very strange decisions. We have sometimes been blinded by our own personal agenda to the point where we think God failed to give us what we thought would make us successful, publicly vindicated, happy and proved to be in the right. This is a form of idolatry, where the little "god" we have chosen to worship is in fact, simply ourselves. We need the Jonah treatment. It often comes in the form of a searching question.

When Jonah had ceased his blustering, God asked him,

"Is it right for you to be angry?" (Jonah 4:4b)

The thrust of the closing section of the book of Jonah is all about God's methods of dealing with the inner motivations of the prophet's heart. Here is a man who had once been at the centre of a king's court, speaking words of wisdom and favour, admired for his eloquent support for his nation. He had known success in his role as God's prophet and even though he had made a mistake and boarded a ship to Tarshish, he was now back on track with God having encountered immense mercy and forgiveness that he did not deserve. In going to Nineveh, he was restored to his former status and divine favour. Surely God would be pleased with his obedience? But this was not the case at all. Jonah had nurtured a recalcitrant, secret, judgemental attitude and God now challenged him about this. He had become trapped by his hardness of heart and his selfish grasp upon God's blessings, having a mental block over God's inappropriate generosity to *the likes of them*. Outrageous!

C.S. Lewis once said, "God is always saving people I don't like, and saving them in a manner I don't wholly approve of!" Whether it is the murderer serving a life sentence in prison or the drug dealer in the murky alleyways of a sprawling city, God will persistently visit people who are in our reckoning, the lowest of the low. He does not reserve salvation for the white, highly educated, more than half-decent upper-middle class. The Azusa Street revival of 1905-6 in California began in a small warehouse in a suburb of Los Angeles and was led by William J Seymour, a one-eyed black pastor who was the son of former slaves. As the Holy Spirit was poured out and miracles abounded, it was the educated white middle class neighbours who not only denounced what was happening, but were deeply offended that God would choose to do such things through such people. *Who does God think He is?*

As heated vengeance bubbles up inside Jonah, God faces him with his pride. The prophet who would rather die than see Nineveh restored is now faced up with the mismatch between his own vision and the vision of the God on whose behalf he speaks. Scripture tells us that God will always look on the heart not on the outward appearance (1 Samuel 16:7). Even though Jonah was still His spokesman in an outward sense, God did not have Jonah's heart allegiance inwardly. When things go wrong on the inside, they eventually manifest on the outside. We have no right to be angry with God if He surprises us with His goodness to people who we deem to be unworthy of it. The cross of Christ is for the salvation of all - men, women and children of every strata and ethnicity. Why should God obey our own personal agendas? Why would He agree with our views about who does and who does not fit the Christian demographic? Unlike Jonah, should we not rejoice when anyone, regardless of colour, race, creed, history, motivation, capability, character or personality enters into the blessing of knowing God's mercy and love? Or perhaps some of us still regard this as outrageous.

The desert bloom, worm and heat

After the announcement was made to Nineveh, Jonah removed himself from the heat of intense repentance to the heat of the surrounding desert. He sat in the sand under his own little makeshift shelter from the hot sun, and waited to see what would happen to the city. Sulking and sweaty, he had positioned himself for a front row seat in the grand finale, which was to be "the end of the world" for Nineveh. What Jonah did not realise was that God's attention was just as much, if not more, on his own life now, rather than on the actions of the Ninevites.

God had a two-fold strategy:

1. The Plant

As the prophet begins to bake in the searing heat of the desert, God attempts to soften Jonah's heart with personal kindness by providing a plant to shield his head. Most translations of the

Bible do not list the specific nature of the plant, but the Revised Standard Version refers to it as a "castor oil" plant. Perhaps this spoke of Jonah's desperate need to be eased from his uptight spiritual constipation! The New International Version calls it "a vine" which could reflect the need for Jonah to once again choose fruitfulness over barrenness in his attitudes to the lost. Either way, Jonah is cooled and relieved by God's mercy and appears grateful for it, so that his big anger is replaced by big gladness (Jonah 4:6).

In reality, however, God wanted to highlight an important fact to Jonah at this point. He was meant to see that each person is in urgent need of relief from distress and the protection of God against the fires of His just destruction. It was necessary for Jonah to understand that if he could not withstand the blaze of the sun without God's mercy, how could the Ninevites withstand the blaze of God's holy wrath? It may have been an act of kindness from God to shield the prophet, but it was also a wake up call for Jonah to think about this in relation to the awful fate of Nineveh, that Jonah had threatened. We all need comfort, shade, pleasure, a much-needed break, good food, pleasant sights, and new places to visit. God often supplies them all – sometimes in ways that display His outrageous kindness.

2. The Worm and the Wind

This time, at first light, God arranges another appointment with Jonah and commands a worm and a wind to arrest him. "But when dawn came up the next day, God appointed a worm that attacked the plant, so that it withered. When the sun rose, God appointed a scorching east wind, and the sun beat down on the head of Jonah so that he was faint." (Jonah 4:7-8a).

The worm is the equivalent of our niggling irritations, sudden set-backs, reversals, losses, and disappointing outcomes. The wind was most likely a fierce sirocco since they are not uncommon in the desert. Such a blast of furnace-hot air not only whips up a sandstorm it also desiccates everything living that happens to be in its path, including people. The plant that had protected him the day before was now withered and the sirocco heat that followed would have been, for Jonah, similar to sitting in the middle of a blast furnace.

Both the worm and the wind were acting on the command of God and Jonah was left in some kind of living hell for the rest of the day, as God slowly turned up the temperature. In effect, God allowed Jonah to taste the torment He had intended for Nineveh prior to God's shocking decision to relent this outcome. The difference was that the people of that city would have lived through all eternity in a worse kind of torment had they died. God was only temporarily facing Jonah with the seriousness of his hardness towards Nineveh, and his self-centred unwillingness to align himself with the mercy of God for that city. Again, Jonah wanted to die! But God would not let him, because He wanted Jonah to contemplate his answer to two pertinent questions that were to follow:

i) "Is it right for you to be angry about the plant?" (Jonah 4:9a NIV). Of course, this question carries an unspoken rider of "...and yet feel nothing about Nineveh?" Jonah's response to God is that he confesses he is extremely angry about the demise of the plant that was there for his protection from the sun. He is consumed by anger; highly offended that God would expose him to such harsh elements in this way. Tragically, all he still cared about was his own comfort, and he failed abysmally to see the parallel with Nineveh. So too, we can respond to similar crisis situations in our lives in the same twisted way. We are more upset if our television breaks down than we are about the salvation of our neighbours. We are totally preoccupied with the loss of our wallet, but only give the welfare of a famine stricken country a fleeting thought perhaps once a year. We cling to our comforts and fail to understand that we have no right to be angry at sudden reversals given the generosity with which God has so consistently treated us. Then comes another poignant enquiry from God.

ii) "And should I not have concern for the great city of Nineveh?" (Jonah 4:11a NIV). The vine was simply the display of a few hours of creative energy and generous benevolent work for God but nevertheless, He told Jonah that He had personally tended it and made it grow. In stark contrast, the Ninevites had taken the accumulated care and attention of God for their welfare over many decades in terms of His love and detailed care to fashion and form them. Each individual was a special project; men, women and children made in His own image. Why, God asks Jonah, should He not care deeply about this huge city when He has tended it through the years – pagans though they were? They may not have known Him or acknowledged His being and greatness in worship until that recent moment when the scales fell from their eyes and they repented, but they had always been His treasure, and now they always would be. The city was teeming with His creation handiwork, which had been sustained by His care and He could not stop loving it now.

Jonah misunderstood the depth of commitment God had for the city He had watched spiral into darkness over many decades. But God cannot switch His affections on and off like some fickle lover, and the same is true today. Across the world, in the reach of His common grace to every tribe, tongue, nation and religion, God remains committed to reveal Himself to them, and display

His love to His hand-made, bespoke people everywhere. This haunting rebuke from God came like the piercing thrust of a sharp sword to challenge the narrow bigotry and hidden racism at the heart of the prophet. The smug, self-satisfied, frigid attitude of this exclusive and bigoted Jewish missionary had been exposed to the heat of God's discerning judgement.

In the same way, God can and will expose each and every one of us to our narrow-minded bigotry concerning our pinched and prejudiced views of who does, and who does not receive His mercy.

God can just as easily, and often does, whether in subtle or more overt ways, ask me the same question concerning the city in which I presently reside:

"Should I not be concerned about this great city of London?" And the same is also true for you in your own village, town or city. Remember, God desperately wants all people to be saved and come to a full knowledge of the truth. There is no room for bigotry in the kingdom of God.

"This is good, and it is pleasing in the sight of God our Saviour, who desires all people to be saved and to come to the knowledge of the truth" (1 Timothy 2:3-4). Hard to believe? Well, He saved you and me didn't He?

There is nowhere to hide

Jonah tried his very best to hide from God but all his rickety shelters were inadequate. Whether he was sleeping deep in the ship's hold, lying under his primitive desert shelter outside the city walls, or believing that a plant would sustain him day after day, nothing could cover him from exposure to God. The only thing that has remotely and wonderfully succeeded around Jonah's botched attempts to outwit God throughout the four short chapters of this striking narrative is the word of God and His life-saving mercy and power extended to lost people.

And finally...

One last enquiry should be on all of our lips. What happened to Jonah? What did he do next? How did he respond to God's treatment? The answer is, we don't know. The stunning art of this narrative and it's ending that isn't an ending, is more like the finale to a French existentialist novel designed to leave us all in the air until we too want to ask all the right questions about what we've read. The book of Jonah does not end happily, except of course for the astonishing revival that came to Nineveh. Instead we have, as Gordon Keddie puts it, "a deeply disturbing and even unsatisfying last chapter."

There is no further recorded interaction between God and His chastened prophet. In fact, Jonah's silence is deafening and we are told nothing more about what Jonah does, where he goes or if God calls him to mission ever again.

No wonder God asks,

"And should I not pity Nineveh, that great city, in which there are more than 120,000 persons who do not know their right hand from their left, and also much cattle?" (Jonah 4:11)

This final question from God is suspended in mid air, leaving us breathless with the realization of his unending commitment to the world He has made. The smallness of Jonah, and his preoccupation with his own welfare as the plant withers, is a far cry from God's generous grace to those 120,000 people in a lawless doomed city. It's time to shift our gaze from Jonah to ourselves. What is your answer to God's final enquiry? We simply don't know what Jonah's was. But he is no longer our concern. It is you and I who are in God's spotlight now.

While we pre-occupy ourselves with minor distractions, God wants to save multitudes presently imperilled in this world, rescue those trafficked in huge numbers all over the world as sex slaves, and call a halt on the premature deaths of children yet unborn. While we concern ourselves with our own comfort, God sends His disturbing presence so that His people rid themselves completely of the Jonah complex and turn their hearts to the lost and spiritually and materially poor who have nothing.

I'm provoked to think of the question God sometimes poses as to how we can sit in our sheltered churches and simply watch our world descend deeper into darkness and death?

How can we look on from a distance from our safe vantage point and not get our hands as dirty as God did in Jesus' descent to earth as the God-man who lived a humbled and sacrificial life of thirty-three years amid third world poverty, human evil, and political turmoil bordering on tyranny?

The cross of Christ is the ultimate expression of God's love for a lost world and following Him requires us to daily take up that cross and learn to lean into His ways, growing into His likeness and adopting His nature and character through the powerful presence of His Holy Spirit.

Our world is a complex place with many needs and appalling tragedies, but contrary to what Jonah initially thought, obedience to the call of God is clear, compelling and simple.

Don't turn away from His mercy and favour in calling each one of us to Himself and then launching us upon our life destiny. Put your hand into His and run into your own special adventure with the God who has so surprisingly rescued you.

Is there anything more important to you than God Himself?

If so, then it is time for all of us to rediscover the outrageous grace of God.

Recommended Reading

Baker, David W., Alexander, T. Desmond. Waltke, Bruce K., Obadiah, Jonah and Micah, Tyndale Old Testament Commentaries, UK, 1988

Briscoe, D. Stuart, *Taking God Seriously*, WORD (UK), 1987

DiGangi, Mariano, *Twelve Prophetic Voices*, Victor Books, USA, 1985

Brueggemann, Walter, *The Prophetic Imagination*, Fortress Press, USA, 1978

Chisholm, Robert B., *Handbook on the Prophets*, Baker Academic, USA, 2002

Fairbairn, Patrick, *Jonah: His Life, Character, Mission*, Baker, USA, 1980

Keddie, Gordon J., *Preacher on the Run*, Evangelical Press, UK, 1986

Kendall, R.T., *Jonah – An Exposition*, Hodder and Stoughton, UK, 1978

Mackay, John L., *God's Just Demands in Jonah Micah Nahum*, Christian Focus, UK, 1993

Morris, Henry M., *The Remarkable Journey of Jonah*, Master Books, USA, 2003

Laetsch, Dr. Theo, *Bible Commentary – The Minor Prophets*, Concordia Publishing, USA, 1956

Nixon, Roesemary, *BST – The Message of Jonah*, IVP, UK, 2003

Peterson, Eugene H., *Under A Predictable Plant*, Eerdmans, USA, 1992